Think NaKed

D1114562

TESTIMONIALS

"The inherent brilliance in children is something we all know about, but howdo you leverage it in the adult world? Read *Think Naked* and you'll find out how!"

— SUE WELLINGTON,
FORMER PRESIDENT OF GATORADE

"If there were a Hall of Fame for books on How to Think, *Think Naked* would be in the front lobby."

— MARTY BRENNAMAN,
BASEBALL HALL OF FAME 2000, *VOICE OF THE CINCINNATI REDS*

"I've been involved in the process of generating new product and packaging ideas for all of my 21-years in the CPG industry, and have seen many tools and techniques over the years. The Think Naked process is, without a doubt, the best. There is simply no other (process), which holds a candle to the *Think Naked* process."

— CHUCK MANISCALCO,
PRESIDENT, GATORADE

"Marco Marsan is inspiration and affirmation of our innate creativity—he's the catalyst that reminds us of what we'd forgotten we could do. I've explored more great ideas over lunch with Marco than in any brainstorming session I've ever attended."

— KENDALL CROLIUS,
FORBES MAGAZINE

"Marco Marsan still thinks like a kid.
And his new book, *Think Naked*, contains the perfect
prescription for bringing your cheeky, childlike
optimism back into your adult life."

— ART LINKLETTER

"If you're 100 percent happy with your life,
very successful, swaddled in an incredibly
loving relationship, if you're having a ball at work
and in the best physical shape possible, if you're
an astute problem solver who's ready for anything
and never in despair, if you're all these things—
then don't touch this book! But if you think you
could take your game up, I guarantee you will
after you read *Think Naked!*"

— PETE BLACKSHAW,
CEO PLANET FEEDBACK

"Marco is a champion at bringing ideas out of your
creative side that you never knew you had."

— SOREN BJORN,
VICE PRESIDENT, DEL MONTE

think NAKED

Childlike Brilliance
in the Rough Adult World

Hi, my name is ...

MarCo MARSaN

with *Peter Lloyd*

JODERE
GROUP
SAN DIEGO, CALIFORNIA

JODERE
GROUP

JODERE GROUP, INC.
P.O. Box 910147, San Diego, CA 92191-0147
800.569.1002 • www.jodere.com

Editorial supervision by Chad Edwards

Library of Congress Cataloging-in-Publication Data

Marsan, Marco.
    Think naked : childlike brilliance in the rough adult world! / Marco Marsan ;
with Peter Lloyd
        p. cm.
            ISBN 1-58872-042-X
        1. Success—Psychological aspects. 2. Success in business. 3. Self-actualization
(Psychology) I. Lloyd, Peter. II. Title.

BF637 .S8 M2873 2003
158.1--dc21

2002035691

ISBN 1-58872-042-X
06 05 04 03   4 3 2 1
First printing, April 2003

PRINTED IN THE UNITED STATES OF AMERICA

Illustrations by GARY KOPERVAS

Book design by CHARLES McSTRAVICK

CONTENTS

PREFACE IX
ACKNOWLEDGMENTS XIII

INTRODUCTION 1

1. YOU WERE A GENIUS 5
Discovering the childlike brilliance you were born with

2. YOU LOST YOUR MARBLES 15
Fear, anxiety, brain efficiency, and adulthood

3. SEE SAW 37
Balancing the combination of kidlike genius
with your adult wealth of experience

4. WEAR YOUR CAPE 45
How to create conditions that encourage
risk-taking without fear

5. BLOCKBUSTER 73
Busting the barriers that block optimism, opportunity,
and success from your life

6. LOOK AT YOUR NEIGHBOR'S PAPER 123
Making the most of smart help, strategic stimulation,
and sage advice

7. SHOW-N-TELL 161
How to get in touch with your passions
and express your exuberance

8. I'M THE BOSS OF ME 205
Developing your Naked Reflex with choice,
responsibility, and daily commitment

ABOUT MARCO MARSAN 227

PREFACE

The purpose of a preface is to engage you in the book you're about to read. It should give you a hook, a quick and simple reason why you should read the book. So here's the hook: Life can suck! Friends and family members die. You could lose your job. Stock prices drop. All kinds of disasters just happen. No warning.

Don't you wish you had what it takes to handle all the crap that life serves up? Well, you do. At least you did. You were once fully equipped to make life an incredible experience. And just having someone tell you this goes a long way toward making your life as rewarding as possible. Let me tell you a story to illustrate my point.

When I was ten years old, my gang of friends could make the difference between a great day and terrible day. If I didn't get to see them, it was a terrible day. When I saw them, it was usually a great day.

We were all best buddies. If you'd cross us, we'd make your life miserable. Worse yet, if anyone of us crossed each other, the gang would get behind one and make life hell for the other. I know, because they made one of my days the most miserable in my life.

In our neighborhood, mothers learned to recognize their sons' friends from the shoulders down. That's because we spent so much time with our heads in their refrigerators. It was usually okay to eat what we wanted at each other's homes. How was I to know Gene's mother had special plans for her marzipan?

Marzipan was new to me, it sounded like "Marsan," and it turned out to be delicious. So I had my fill while I waited for Gene to come down from his room. Big mistake. The moment I saw him, I knew I was in trouble. He chased me out his back door into his yard, where we argued until I realized it was useless to reason with him. His mom was going to be furious with him and I was his scapegoat.

I went home dejected and hung out in my room. My mom was in the kitchen when I heard Gene with all our friends outside. "Hey, Marco, you want some marzipan? We brought some for you. In case you didn't get enough." They were out for blood. When I didn't answer, their taunts got more severe.

"That was really stupid, Marco. You're really dumb. Come out and get some more marzipan, Marsan. Eat some more, moron." They weren't about to let me off. My stomach turned the marzipan over a few times. These guys were my world. Now they were all against me. I couldn't feel more alone and embarrassed.

My mom asked, "What's going on?" in her wonderfully lyrical, Italian accent. I pretended not to know, but she saw right through me. She could feel my fear and rejection. As the taunts continued, her face took on a fierceness I had never seen. Something they were saying struck and deeply hurt her.

In the most dignified yet forceful way, she stepped outside, one hand on her hip, the other wagging her finger, "You boys don't know what you're saying," she scolded in broken English. "Marco was tested as a genius at the University of Chicago. Nobody's stupid. You're being mean and I've had enough. Go home or I'll call your parents." They scattered.

I was impressed with my mother's power over my friends, but I sat alone, puzzled, scrunching my eyebrows. Genius? Where did that come from? Did she just make it up? University of Chicago? Was I really a genius? I loved the idea, but wondered if it was true. Unfortunately, I didn't ask.

We now know that when teachers or parents treat children as if they are gifted, the children tend to live up to that expectation. As you'd expect, the opposite is true. Treat kids like they're stupid and they tend to act that way. You can understand why the taunts of my friends had set her off.

Fast-forward 20 years—dinner at my parents' house. My sister is serving marzipan. I look at my mother across the table. "Mom, remember the time I ate the marzipan at Gene's house? I want you to know how much I appreciate the way you stood up for me that day, and that University of Chicago genius story. That was a real nice touch."

After a pregnant pause, my mother stood up and took me by the shoulders. Her eyes welled with tears as she told me, "Tesoro! La storia è vero!" (Sweetheart! The story is true.) She explained that as a four-year-old, I was a prolific block builder, puzzle solver, and prodigiously expressive. So she and my dad took me to the University of Chicago when I was four and had me tested—IQ 152!

It was as if I had been punched in the gut; I didn't know how to react. I was exhilarated! Yes! I'm a genius, or at least I was. Wait! Should I be happy or pissed? What if I had known of my gift? Would it have changed me, changed the way I approached life? The way I solved problems? How would I have handled all of those trying times? How would others have treated me knowing I was a genius? Why did I have to wait till I was in my thirties to find out? I wouldn't have felt like such a nimrod for so many years. I couldn't keep the tears from my eyes. I felt relieved and empowered, but also a bit betrayed that I hadn't heard sooner.

From that day, I began developing my Think Naked principles. I learned that 98 percent of us are geniuses early in life. And almost all of us lose it. Is it lost forever? Can we recapture our childhood brilliance? This book will prove that the answer is yes. Better yet, if we put the sum of our life of experience in the hands of our four-year-old genius, we can lead fuller and more satisfying lives than we ever thought possible.

Don't doubt it any longer. I'm telling you now. You were a genius. And we're going to get it back. By the time you finish this book, you're going to enjoy the same exhilaration I felt when my mother, looked me in the eyes and promised, "Tesoro. La storia è vero!"

ACKNOWLEDGMENTS

TO MY FAMILY

Mario, the inventive, anarchistic force that is MARSAN; Maria, who epitomizes the respectability and necessity of motherhood; my son, Shane, my greatest gift in life, and to Kathy for bestowing him on me; Steve, my unconditional friend, the brilliant engineer and smile in my life; Richard, devotion, passion, doing the right thing; Tyler, Sarah, Michael, Matthew, Leah, the most amazing nieces and nephews; Laura, Kathi, Kimarie; the next generation of American women; and to the rest of my family—reminders of my roots, proof of the enormity of the human spirit: Giorgio, Gino, Andrea, Guerrino, Sylvie, Nadia, Stephanie, Erica, Antonio, Shirley, Franco, BJ, Renato, Louisa, Marco, Luigino, Edda, Inelda

TO THE MARCO POLO EXPLORERS

Jim Tobergta, whose spirit, knowledge and skill refresh the world; Wendi Ezgur, you could eat a pie off her grandmother's head; Sandie Glass, insight and pragmatism in one; Teresa Herd, friend, confidante and Duran Duran fan; Gary Kopervas, who inspired the book title and lives life naked; Steve Merino, contemporary and hilarious, a renaissance man; Chris Breen, William Burroughs without the sordid past; Christine Carter, try to be stern-faced around her, not possible; Dawn Cariello, off-color comment queen and you love her for it; Kari White, for her grace under fire and her incredible artistic ideals; Marianne Pontillo, the smartest, hottest, most articulate, eligible woman in Philly; Jon Harcharak, a lovely man, father, who can do pull-ups with two fingers; Sherry Scull, a joyful, intelligent, beautiful, smart, shall I continue?; Steve Wuesthoff; Fun, Freak, Fluid, Fantastic and a bunch of other f-words; Tai Duncan, her zest for life messes with anyone considering adulthood; Mike Farrell, in the trenches, living the life and translating it for the wannabes; Dr. Cheri Anderson, highest level of Insight in bite-size pieces—she's brilliant; Ingrid Nagy, the inspiration for the company Marco Polo Explorers; Tony Guard, words cannot describe his talent, an icon of fatherhood; Lori Lafferty, goodness personified, an amazing teammate; Peter Lloyd, a think naked icon, this book would not have happened if it weren't for his devotion, passion, exuberance and skill; Debbie Luican, for her faith, vision and capitalistic altruism.

To those who've left
a positive imprint on my DNA

Randi Baremore; Chris Taylor; Tom Massey; George Prince; Mark Levinson; David Germano; Michelle Treadway; Art Linkletter; Tommie Smith; Sam Wych; The Pennos; Andrew Gohr; John Savidge; Miro Odic; Leo Buscaglia; Barbara Lazaroff; Judith Lloyd ("For unwavering love support and encouragement." — Peter); for editing our book with painless passion, Chad Edwards; for his incredible art direction, Charles McStravick; for demonstrating the power of the cape, David Lloyd and John Pferdmenges.

ACKNOWLEDGMENTS

University of Cincinnati students

Scott Whitlock, Diane Burke, Jodi Heyman, Jennifer Bahrs

People I'd sit next to during a test

Dan Runk, Bill Paulin, Bill Posey, Tony Arrasmith, Feryal Khan, Dr. Bruce Corser, Leslie Huesman, Pamela Dory, Dave Burwick

Professional advice and encouragement (Peter)

Steve Grossman, Jerry Malsh, Gabrielle Fox, Andy van Gundy, Michael Michalko, Tim Hurson, Roger von Oech

Habla Blah Blah Contributors

Richard Marsan, Caitlyn Lloyd, Koko the Gorilla, Aidan Ezgur, Jim Tobergta, Anton Blignaut

Special thanks to

Doug Hall, and Dick from Big Co.

TWO DEGREES

Montserrat Petit • Shephali Patel • André 3000 • Mitch Sisskind • Gary Philbin • Joy Behar • 7
Pecora • Jeff Rogers • Tara Snodgrass • Linda Roberts • Larry Sheakley • The Westermeyers •
• Tom Durban • Joy Browning • Sierra Mist 8-3-03 • Chris Rock • Dennis Miller • Lauren Hill • Le
ziata • Tracy Bender • Terry Bryan • Elizabeth & Brooklyn Blackmore • Hubert and Irma Beut
Rachel Ellis • Ted Woehrle • Steve Franz • Karen Gralnek • Demetrius Fuller • Ling Lucas • Robi
Lisa Law • Jeff Landis • Nathan Coleman • Mark Schooner • Brett Dickson • Ernesto Levy • Mik
• Lisa Ling • Mary Hall • Jim Norgren • Donna Liebold • Ed Winter • Lee Iacocca • John Beltz •
• Jimmy Gherardi • Claire Farber • Bill Vernick • Diane Iseman • Dr. Sandy Goldberg •
Hitzel • Kirk Hodgdon • Mike Wilt • Kim Portrate • Art Rosenberg • Rowena Alston • Angela
McKinney • Mary Holt • Mary Ellen Vicksta • Rhonda Harper • Pat Collins • Jeff Mordos • Mary
Wilhelmi • Bill Tennant • Chris Mahoney • Susan Rubin • Joe Gardner • Gigi Pavelec • Merilee M
Maniscalco • Dave Schowalter • Katie Lacey • Marisol Tamaro • Dan Spangler • Kelly Regan • S
• Liz Mohr • Lauren Hobart • Jill Pratt • Peter Baker • Blue 32 • Mike McGowan • Patty Newe
Bowyer • Alexis Cosse • Rob Weicke • Michael Lancor • Deborah Candeub • Harry Dent • Pete
Snelling • Roger Frye • Tim Heaviside • Tracy Minder • Lew Goldstein • Julie Templeton • Paul K
• Marison Sanchez • Jennifer Spainhour • Bobby Williams • Tom Bene • Carol Watzke • Victoria M
• Terri Polk • Julie Newhouse Goldman • Brian Lembke • Joel Goodman • Reetu Agarwala • M
Neff • Annie Kim • Muriel Nellis • Elizabeth Davis • Nancy Davidson • Tom Hernquist • Jim O'Conn
• Kim Thomsen • Emilie Kendall • Renelle Russell • Paula Farrington • Lara Kudryk Traska • D
merman • Lisa Barrios • Art DeCesaro • Shawn Budde • Jan Klawans • Sally Burnett • Imre An
Steve Prod • John Galloway • Brad Claypool • Robert Speranza • Rachana Bhatt • Josie Well
Indra Nooyi • Opokua Kwapong • Julia Tuthill • Jamie Shuttleworth • Gretchen Mueller • Greg
Nicholson • Charlee Taylor-Hanes • Don Scheibenreis • Becky Caldwell • Scott Moffit • Dirk Cot
• Ben DeSanti • Lisa Chancellor • Sharon Dickinson • Jennifer Stephens • Art Anderson • Chris
• David Dahlman • Stephen Lee • Stacy Reichert • Susan Serge • Craig Braasch • Neal Stamme
• Brendan Boyle • Mike Dillon • Gavin Blawie • Kirk Bryans • Ron Bryar • James Miller • Stacey
Reynolds • Linda Seacord • Cheryl LaJeunesse • Dave Buklarewicz • Jocelyn Mallory • Anne S
Mardula • Craig Northrup • Brian Van Houten • Suzanne Kolb • Tim Titus • Pete Lewis • Laurie
Valerie Totty • Lynne Jones • Marc Johnston • Cheri Miller • Alpa Pandya • Jon Grondahl • Gler
Linck • Devery Holmes • Craig Coffey • Robert Smith • Miki Tsusaka • Joe Bock • Alice Wallac
Yocum • John Andrukonis • Tom Palmer • Megan Pryor • Jershon Jones • Matt Seiler • Dan Tere
Katz • Tina Counts • Helen Roth Bassel • Bob Bibb • Lee Anne Gardner • Eva Niewadowiski • .
Susan Shields • Carey Kyler • Oz Parvaiz • Meena Mansharamani • Ursula O'Donavan • Jim Dw
Schoster • Cathy Bertke • Rev. Damon Lynch • Danielle Crane • Kristin Everett • Frida Depaz
Killeen • Steve Malone • Penelope Finnie • Patty Newcomer-Simmons • Marti Morfitt • Lynn Bru
• Claudio Stemberger • Tom Gooch • Mark Misiano • Ruby Kirkup • June Devalk • Dawn Houghton • Chr
• Michael Johnson • Mike McNamara • Doc Bullard • Julie Cary • Anna Mulock Houwer • Page Lewis
Gurian • James Nyce • Chris Sisler • Jonathan Weiner • Joyce Lizzi • Susan Mahler • Phil Profitt • La
• Tia Maria Smith • Ted Manley • Deborah Grassi • Mark Micacich • Pam Taylor • James Riggs • St

ACKNOWLEDGMENTS

OF SEPARATION

...eiers • Ray Nealon • Becky Yosafat • Kim Watling • Sarah Bellamy • Bruce Chatterley • Karin
...mbrodt • Bob Rinaldi • Chuck D • Sue Wellington • Wolfgang Puck • Marisa Tomei • Randy Geller
...• Travis Funk • Roger Berdusco • Frida Depaz • Rosa Blasi • Eric Nies • Sona Bhatt • Sue Annun-
...Amy Elliott Hemeter • Jeff Immelt • Kathleen Wallstein • Brian Dudley • Dr. Rochelle Wainer •
...• Bob Taraschi • Ezzy Languzzi • Connie Williams • Regina Kulik • Walter Leaphart • Chris and
...Kai Mbayo • Jamie Lehman • Denny McCaughey • Ramon Arguedas • David James • Jamie Intile
...lay • Jeff Martin • Paul Racicot • Vicki Swanson • Gary Rodkin • Jay Waddell • Gayle Franger
...ke • Bunny French • Dave Nolletti • Mark Lantz • Janice Weiss • Mitch Meyers • John
...auren Radossich • Jerry Knight • Kelly Hsieh • Lesley Pfitzenmeyer • Susan Haunschild • Chris
...Robyn Schauweker • Lon Schwear • Sue Franz • Jon Rasich • Jaime Vasquez • Al Klein • Gary
...Wylie Schwieder • Vera Holroyd • Steve Dunphy • Angelique Bellmer • Kathy Mulcahy • Chuck
...rson • Jake Van Wyke • Jim Sexton • John Bretz • Scott Osiecki • Joanne Hogan • Dennis Ready
...mmons • Rob Demars • Francis Britchford • Rose Noesges • Geoffroy Van Raemdonck • Heather
...w • Michael Leifer • Dawn Hudson • Mike Mahoney • Carrie Koberstein • Kris Ellenberg • Tim
...nja Borris • Christine Sisler • Beverley Guyer • Tom Smallhorn • Andee Wilkov • Marion Dalaker
...este • Amy Scott • Noel Anderson • Lou Imbrogno • Tanuja Singeetham • Al Bolles • Scott Hughes
...v • Gary Carder • Guiseppe D'Alessandro • Shephali Patel • Cathy Maas • Mindy Mullins • Jack
...Kearns • Jeff Wolfson • Katie Latimer • Matt Nelson • Joe Reinstein • Ron Weiss • Marc Speiker
...• Soren Bjorn • Pam VanIngen • Dawn Chapman • Laura Bench • Harvey Briggs • Robert Zim-
...antyus • Henry Vogel • Eric Powders • Jennifer Boehlke • Arla Gomberg • Stephanie Feaster •
...Schuler • Cat Payne • Shailender Khitri • Jeff Myers • Elizabeth Marshall • Russell Weiner •
...ff Fisher • Pam Crain • David Dalton • Lucinda Styne • Steve Astephen • Karin Danganan • Cie
...• Donna Covrett • Patty Bain • Tracy Russell • Katie Dadagian • Rick Langan • Margaret Steele
...ki • Erika Brown • Mike Venne • Ken Rusche • Harvey Hunerberg • Becky Ingis • Lisa Francella
...opaz • David Johnston • Rich Egge • Amy Chang • Derek Arzoo • Julie Barrett • Deborah Hicks
...• Scott Hildebrand • Chris Constello • Heidi Sandreuter • Deepak Masand • Tony Dieste • Kathy
...Mike Payne • Tim Hawley • Cara Hunter • Cory Basso • Bobby Merkel • Lynn Kuzina • Rebbeca
...anne Haase • Haley Rubin • Jeff Van Hanswyk • Leonid Sudakov • Deb Fifles • Bill McDonald •
...• Susan Leen • Elizabeth Friedman • Marie Guerra • Kristina Bullard • Jacqueline Rivera • Troy
...arker • Gerard Lafond • Chris Kitson • Tess Resman • Wayne Carpenter • Rick Shepard • Paul
...Gies • Steven Quinn • Kevin Hochman • Massimo D'Amore • Phil Klein • Minje Martinez • Bruce
...ia • Van Sapp • Ellen Furuya • Suzanne Lang • Cathy Kapica • Ellen Ginty • John McClintock •
...Butler • Patrick Reynolds • Mary Yuan • Gena Poynter • Jerry Dehner • Bill Crossett • Adam
...orkum • Jourdan Zayles • Kenddra Munchel • Kenyatta Nelson • Leslie at the Strand • Liam
...• Wells • Seth Godin • Ron Lieber • Margot Davis • Tim Pascoe • Tim Zimmerman • Susan Lapointe
...Kinney • Elena Kanner • Christine Prociv • Sheila Teahan • Don Becker • Cristina Garcia • Mark Noonan
...rell • Katie Davis • Lisa Erspamer • Allison Krauss • Jack Mori • Ellen Rakleten • Dawn Bartels • Sonj
...• Brenda Murphy • Esi Eggleston • Cindy Alston • Katie Bartholomew • Karin Gralnek • Shalini Gupta
...ke • Janice Faison • Jeffrey Wolfson • Chris Allen • Doug Zalla • Anna Gaffney • Jeffery Rogers

INTRODUCTION

This book explores the world of the child, what they do without even blinking an eye, the purity of their genius and the principles that drive their imaginative life. It operates on the premise that, if we could think as nimbly as a child and combine that power with our adult library of knowledge, we can achieve life and world-changing breakthroughs!

To help bring home the purity of childlike genius, I wrote this book naked. No, not literally. I gave my four-year-old genius control of my wiring. The book presents a lot of its material the way a kid would. If it were a coloring book, my colors would go outside the lines. It's organized like a kid's room. You should read it that way. Look around and go to what piques your interest. Start it but never finish it. Keep it near you, contemplate its principles, apply them to specific problems, but never stop going back to it.

Some people find it helpful to keep a checklist or a journal of their progress. If you think this will help you consciously commit yourself to your Think Naked program, then do it. Do whatever it takes to make and continually reinforce your commitment.

You may read a passage and shake your head in amazement. Some of the facts I've dug up really are pretty amazing. I've done my level best to check and double-check all my facts. Of course, new research bumps aside older facts all the time. So, as they say in the commercials, "Don't take my word for it." If something sounds fishy, listen to your four-year-old when it says, "Nuh-uh!" and check my facts. You're sure to find something interesting and helpful even if you don't prove me wrong.

Throughout our journey back to when you were at your best, we'll be making a number of turns and unexpected detours in order for me to make my points. In every chapter, when I make a point, I'll be as clear and direct as possible. Each point supports a principle. Each principle has a kidlike name but it's backed by the best adult substantiation I could find. I've included practical techniques for incorporating each principle into your life. Read and try as many techniques as you like. Try them on a real problem in your life.

Along the side of the road, you'll see optional information in boxes we call sidebars. Read these along with the text or save them for later.

Some chapters contain exercises. Each exercise is designed to help you undo years of negative conditioning. So do them in a very deliberate way. They'll not only help you understand the technique they demonstrate, they'll get you used to thinking naked. At first, it might feel odd or unnatural, like you're acting a little foolish. But gradually, doing the exercises will start to feel quite natural.

In any case, thinking naked will take a good deal of commitment. Without thinking, you've continuously committed yourself to thinking like an adult. You'll have to consciously check the impulse to reject childlike thinking as you read this book. But the more you read and make the new Think Naked principles part of your life, you'll see the inadequacy of the way you've been thinking. You'll see it in yourself and in others.

After all, naked thinking is a way of life. You'll get results on purpose rather than by accident. And you'll learn how to recognize the results that do pop up by accident. Thinking naked will make it so you always have possibilities. With possibilities come more choices, and with more choices, better decisions. It's that simple. You'll never find yourself in a desperate situation again. Those moments that cause you pain or acid indigestion will come less often and present smaller hurdles when they do come. Instead, you'll gradually find yourself handling problems that used to debilitate you.

A word of advice—you might want to have an explanation ready for when your friends or family try to have you locked up. If you see them nodding their heads, feigning understanding, make sure they don't run off and call 911. When they tell you, you've lost it, explain that it's just the opposite. You've found the road back to your childlike genius! Eventually they'll appreciate the difference.

The change in you will be more seamless if you introduce the Think Naked way, little by little, every day into your personal and professional life. People will still notice the more gradual improvement in your ability to create. And I'm not talking about creative as in the creative art of finger painting. No, you'll be more creative as a creator of solutions, new ways to look at the world, new ways to solve everyday problems, new ways to surprise your spouse. Best of all, you'll come to realize that you've never lost your childlike genius!

1

YOU WERE A GENIUS

Every child is an artist. The problem is how to remain an artist after he grows up.

— PABLO PICASSO

What if I could promise you a better life? I mean guarantee you a life full of optimism, opportunity, and success—the ability to navigate through a great life free of fear, embarrassment, and despair. Would you want it? Of course!

What if I told you that you had this ability as a kid but lost it?

It's true! Study after study has proven it. But you knew that. Look at any four-year-old. Check out that Cheshire cat smile. They've got life canned and you don't.

Children are relentlessly curious, eager to explore, and less concerned with limitations than with possibilities. Like adult creative giants, children possess an instinct for creative thinking, for seeing the world in a way that too many of us have completely forgotten.

Can you remember some of the great sensations of your childhood: the feelings, sounds, smells, your pets, favorite toys, neighborhood, bedroom, backyard? Going over to a friend's house, playing games, running around the neighborhood together, and catching lightning bugs. Doing whatever the heck you wanted to for a good part of every day.

Everybody wants to do what he or she wants to do, but that urge was never as strong as when you were a child. You rebelled at having to finish your cooked carrots, do your homework, or come home by dark. Even if it was for your own good, like wearing a coat in cold weather or shoes to cross the street, you complained. And you didn't appreciate coats or shoes until you came in shivering or stepped on a piece of glass.

Now hold those memories! They contain the attitude and feelings you need to rediscover in order to think naked again. Just because you've grown up doesn't mean you have to lose your child-hood genius and resign yourself to the drudgery of day-in-day-out responsibilities. Maybe a story from my life will illustrate a way to grow up without losing your ability to think naked.

HOW I BECAME A NAKED THINKER

I began life like you, as a creative genius. And I might have lost it, if not for my parents, a pair of life-loving Italian immigrants. One day I tested the limits of their love when I dipped my hand into my chocolate pudding and happily began to produce a monochromatic fresco on the kitchen wall. Instead of slapping my hands, my parents heaped praise upon their budding Michelangelo.

My father washed the kitchen walls while my mother celebrated my first masterpiece with cascades of praise. After thoroughly bathing her young artist, she yielded to my irrepressible exuberance and gave me the ultimate reward. Lifting me out of the tub, she turned me loose, naked, and dripping wet, to tear through the house.

Pretending that I had escaped, she called my dad to join the chase. Squealing with glee, I soon found myself cornered on the living room couch. In a blind burst of benign defiance, I charged between my two laughing parents as they continued the chase.

I still try to run with the same spirit of the naked chase—the freedom, the sense of accomplishment, the unrestrained celebration, and the unlimited possibilities. And I want you to find the same kind of excitement and exuberance in your life. To tap into your memory and relive what it was like to think naked. More importantly, I want you to try to put the power of that uninhibited thinking behind all the knowledge and experience of your life.

Naturally, like you, I soon learned that not all adults appreciate naked exuberance. Despite my high IQ, my schoolteachers consistently saw my spirited behavior as a disciplinary problem. I thought the principal's office was where every kid went at least once a day. When I was 17, my career counselor told me I'd do better changing oil instead of pursuing college. Not too many years later the Mazda Corporation named me one of America's top Out-of-the-Box Thinkers. (So my counselor was partly right, because Mazda changes a lot of oil.)

Mazda and a slew of other *Fortune* 500 companies recognized the work I do with my company, Marco Polo Explorers. We put into practice the principles I've set down in this book. My clients call these principles *radical ideation techniques*. Even though these principles have helped create a ton of successful new products and services, they're very simple and not that radical. They all boil down to thinking naked, the way you did as a kid.

TEACHING AWAY GENIUS

You may have seen the extensive George Land studies that proved there was a 98 percent chance you were once a creative genius before age four.

In the early days of the Headstart Program, 1,600 five-year-olds were given a series of standardized tests designed to measure creative thinking. The first round of tests were administered when the kids were three to five years of age. At that point, 98 percent of them scored in the genius category. Five years later the same children took identical tests. Only 32 percent scored in the genius range. Five years later only ten percent scored as well. Since then more than 200,000 adults over the age of 25 have taken the same tests. Only two percent managed to score at the genius level.

Maybe you've read the research by Business Week magazine, which came to similar conclusions about the trajectory of our creative powers—a 40-year-old adult is about two percent as creative as a five-year-old child. No wonder Dr. Seuss once described adults as "obsolete children."

Findings like these tell us that creative genius isn't something you find. It's something you've lost. In fact, the similarities between children and adults we call creative geniuses tell us that people who don't think like children have lost a great treasure. And here's the sad part—you didn't have to lose it. In Land's own words, "non-creative behavior is learned." That's right. If your creative genius had not been beaten out of you by the rules and regulations of a school system designed to produce workers for the Industrial Revolution, you'd still have it.

HOW THIS BOOK CAN HELP YOU

I believe we all have the spirit of our childhood buried deep within and we simply need to release it. This spirit is pure and innocent. When children do things, they are driven by an innocent single-mindedness and pure intent—little, if any, consideration for the consequences. I'm not saying every action of every child shines perfectly pure. I do want us to appreciate, though, the commitment to one intent and the ability to stay focused on that intent.

Remember how much clearer things were as a kid? How when you got up in the morning, you knew what you wanted to do. There was no schedule shuffling. You woke, you played, you ate, you played, you snacked, you played, you napped, you played, you ate, you played, and you crashed.

Can your life ever be that simple again? No. But you can regain the same purity of intent. No more, "should I do this or that?" With purity of intent, you always know what to do. No more fretting over doing what you want to do versus what you have to do. Face it; you never want to do what you have to do. But you've been told you have to do it anyway. I'm here to tell you the reverse is true. You have to do what you want to do. Let's start by discovering what you really want to do—what will make you passionate.

So what do you want to be when you grow up? Are you doing it already? If not, what will drive you toward what you want to be? (Not just once, but everyday, and especially on those days your train jumps the tracks.) Finding out what to be is a big step. Successfully completing it will do wonders. We'll take this step later in the book after we've gone over the principles you need to make that decision with the pure intent of a four-year-old.

I will introduce you to four, easy to apply principles that will shake you out of your adult thinking patterns and empower you to flourish and excel using your natural born, childlike brilliance. These Think Naked principles follow the strategy you'd find in a serious bodybuilding program. Which makes sense. After all, we're rebuilding the most important and powerful part of your body—your brain.

We'll begin by laying a solid foundation, which will provide a mental environment conducive to thinking naked. That's why the first principle, *Wear Your Cape*, attacks fear—the main enemy of your childlike mental agility. It takes some guts to think and act a little differently than the fear-ridden adults around you. I'll give you easy techniques for quieting the fear that naturally comes with taking these risks.

Next, we want to develop stronger, nimbler ways of thinking. So we have to eliminate weak ways of thinking. That means tearing down your tired, adult thinking habits. The second principle, *Blockbuster*, goes after the numskull, adult assumption that just because, "That's how we've always done it," we have to keep doing it that way. I'll show you how to destroy conventional thinking, break stereotypes, challenge authority, and change the rules. Eliminating these barriers will help you get out of your rut and on with a great life.

The third principle, *Look at Your Neighbor's Paper*, asks you to admit, first, that you don't know everything. Second, that in most cases it's perfectly okay to get help—smart help, strategic stimulation, sage advice. In short, to cheat! Or think of it as stacking the deck. Even though you're creative enough to do so, there's no use reinventing the wheel. Instead we'll put some proven "wheels" to work. I'll introduce you to simple and effective tools and techniques that will liberate the way you process information and make you a lean and mean, naked thinking machine. You'll never be without the necessary stimulation to create solid solutions.

In the fourth principle, *Show-N-Tell*, I'll show you how to get in touch with what makes you passionate. If there's one thing that separates ordinary lives from exceptional ones, it's passion—guts, heart, piss and vinegar—the stuff that drives some people to live their dreams without compromise or apology. If you follow the first three principles, you can build an incredibly nimble mind. If you maintain it with exercise, you'll rid yourself of fear and despair. But if you express yourself every day, personal greatness awaits you!

I conclude the book with *I'm the Boss of Me*. Not exactly a principle, but a final call for developing your Naked Reflex. That means making naked thinking something you do without even thinking about it. I'll ask you to choose and make a commitment to the naked thinking way of life throughout the book. In this chapter, however, I'll show you how to think naked without thinking twice. If you can do that, it will mean more opportunities in your future and eventually greater fulfillment in your life and relationships and ultimately a life free of despair.

HELP YOURSELF

Do you realize you just decided to read on? I'd like you to be aware of that. Very aware. Choice is that subtle and it happens every minute. When I talk about how this book can help you, I make that promise with the understanding that you're going to make a choice—the choice to make naked thinking a way of life. I'm not talking about coming to a major intersection and turning north. You need to decide repeatedly to invest

> None
> of the secrets
> of success
> will work
> unless you do.
> — FORTUNE COOKIE

time and energy toward your new way of thinking. Every step along the road is a choice.

Now before you rip off all of your clothes and go running naked through your office or neighborhood, at least read the next chapter.

2

YOU LOST YOUR MARBLES

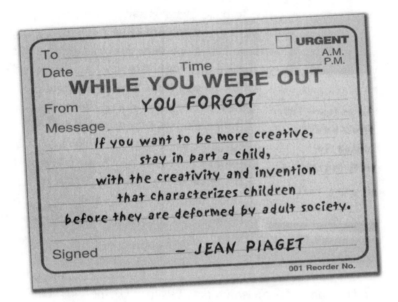

To _____ ☐ **URGENT**

                             A.M.

Date _____ Time _____ P.M.

WHILE YOU WERE OUT

From _____ *YOU FORGOT* _____

Message _____

If you want to be more creative,
stay in part a child,
with the creativity and invention
that characterizes children
before they are deformed by adult society.

Signed _____ — *JEAN PIAGET* _____

001 Reorder No.

THE MEMO

This story is absolutely true. I've not included real names, in order to protect the guilty. As you know by now, Marco Polo Explorers employ the Think Naked philosophy. That's how we remain successful. We try to stack the deck on every project we work on, and we work with the top companies on the planet (I'm not going to namedrop, but seriously some of the greatest brands).

On a recent project guided by Jane, a courageous, high-ranking marketing executive, I visited the corporate offices of (let's just call it) Large Co. I was there to initiate our Discovery process, a comprehensive assessment of the opportunities and challenges the company currently faced. Discovery precedes every project, in part, to create a comfort level among everyone involved. My job that day was to convince the top brass at Large Co. that our team could create new ways to build their consumer base.

I walked into my first meeting with (let's call him) Dick, a senior VP. It was supposed to be a one-on-one, but three of his VPs flanked him as I arrived at 8:30 in the morning. They had had their coffee. It was obvious they had been properly briefed. Dick sat waiting for me with his arms folded. He looked like Torquemada at the Spanish Inquisition, except he and his henchmen weren't wearing red.

Feeling utterly intimidated, I rode my heels for the first three to five minutes, letting the situation get the better of me. Gradually, I got into my groove, with pure intent, trying to understand their business, their competencies and challenges, and began to help them uncover new opportunities. I felt I was doing fine.

Still, as I worked with them, I could feel Dick looking at me funny (and not funny ha-ha). He just didn't seem to like me. No problem. That's his right. But it was more than that. With his body language, he seemed to be telling me that I was keeping him from getting other more important things done; that I was wasting the first hour of his day, that it was personal, and he was going to give me nothing more than the lowest common denominator of respect.

Eventually the torture ended. A few hours later Jane received this memo from Dick:

To __Jane_____ ☐ **URGENT**

Date _____ Time _____ A.M.
P.M.

MEMORANDUM

From __Dick_____

Message _____

REASONS WHY WE SHOULD NOT WORK
WITH MARCO MARSAN
AND MARCO POLO EXPLORERS:

1. There are no new ideas, I've worked in this business for 30 years and we've tried it all.

2. An outsider doesn't know the complexity of our business.

3. Marco Marsan said the word shit in our meeting.

4. I don't like his hair.

Signed _____

#7-92001 Reorder No.

Imagine if I had been introduced to this dude in a sandbox setting or on the beach, both of us in shorts, with our pails and shovels, both four-years-old. There's no way he'd react the same way. If he could have written a memo back then, it might have read like this:

☐ **URGENT**

To __Jane__   A.M.
P.M.

Date _____ Time _____

MEMORANDUM

From __Dick__

Message _____

1. Hey, Jane, Marco's fun!

2. I wanna go to his house!

3. I learned a new word for doo-doo!

4. How does he make his hair stick up all over?

Signed _____

#7-92001 Reorder No.

What happened to Dick over the past 50 years? What made him fear new ideas, outsiders, off-color words, and contemporary haircuts? When did his job become rejecting things he chooses not to understand? What made it personal?

DICK LOST HIS MARBLES

Marbles are cool. They're smooth, shiny, and colorful. They click and roll. And they're fun to collect. In this chapter, marbles represent your active neurons, the brain cells you still use. If you collected marbles as a kid, you've no doubt abandoned them, just as you've stopped using many of your neurons.

Losing your marbles occurs naturally. Much of the loss is out of your control. You don't lose your marbles because you're crazy or deficient. You lose them because growing up systematically breaks down your innate problem solving skills. You lose marbles every day. All around you, people are losing theirs. It's difficult to reverse this attrition.

As we lose our marbles, we can't help but unconsciously encourage others to lose theirs. In a contagious process sort of like yawning, we tend to modify our thinking to the way the people around us think. It's a natural part of getting along with others. It builds affinity and cooperation in groups. Notice how every group develops its own jargon, dress code, and mannerisms. Becoming part of a group is a necessary part of social development.

Belonging to a group is not all bad news. We pick up good thinking habits if we associate with bright, creative people, but unfortunately, these people don't make up the majority. Most people and their lazy, conventional ways of thinking wear down our childlike thinking powers over time. And we help them.

When a work-shirking colleague makes our job more difficult, we often accept their incompetence and work harder to make up for their shortcomings. Every time a surly clerk or moody waiter makes life miserable for us and we take it, our distaste for happily interacting with people increases. Every uncaring doctor, uninvolved counselor, testy teacher, bully cop, insensitive spouse, and all the just plain "mean people" we encounter wear down our optimism.

As a result, we lose the connections—the marbles we had as kids—when our parents, neighbors, relatives, and early teachers "oohed and ahhed," and praised and applauded our every move. We gradually accept the idea that we're just one of many unimportant people in this great, big world. We solidify this idea by actively accepting such a verdict.

We can reverse this process of marble wasting with a concerted, conscious effort. Instead of accepting the daily onslaught of negative messages, you can consciously resist and retain the marbles you've got and regain the ones you've lost. As you do, you gradually re-connect the neurons, recollect the marbles, and rebuild the brain that made you a four-year-old creative genius.

Let me remind you again what a genius you were back then. You learned a new language before you were two! (Try that now.) You learned how to crawl, stand, and walk. You learned how to do things you never thought you could do. You were fluid in the way you approached your day. You took chances you'd never ever consider taking again.

Here's the good news. You can get your marbles back. We'll start by understanding what chased our marbles away. Then you'll be one step closer to regressing to the purity of your childhood.

FEAR

When fear kicks in, an unmistakable alarm rings out to your entire body from a part of the brain known as the amygdala. Your hair stands on end, your heart beats faster, you breathe harder and deeper, and your pupils dilate. In response to the most severe kinds of fear, you scream, punch, or run like crazy from whatever frightens you.

Okay now this is going to freak you out. The same signal—not just a milder version of it, but the same signal that makes you sweat, punch, or run—goes off when someone tells you, "No!" or "Wrong answer!" or "You idiot!" A good verbal flailing is very similar to seeing a ghost, a tiger in the wild, or getting your butt kicked.

Milder whoopings may do even more damage. "You're no Einstein." Has anyone ever said that to you? How did it make you feel? Did it knock you down to size; diminish your spirit a bit? You bet it did. Maybe it was meant to take a little wind out of your sails. (I wonder, why take the wind out of anyone's sails?) What happens to your resolve when someone does? At first, maybe very little. But start piling on whoopings and, over time, we develop such revulsion for being wrong and embarrassed that we become profoundly inhibited. Eventually it can keep us from doing things we know we can do. We learn over time that the surefire way to stop the pummeling is to never be wrong. In other words, be right at all costs or keep your mouth shut.

Ultimately after years of acquiescing, we relegate our heart and mind to a personal purgatory, a place where dreams are put on hold, in exchange for a life of mediocrity and safety.

HARDWIRING

In order to get a picture of how your brain gets hardwired and what's wrong with that, imagine your brain as a tank of marbles. Each marble stands for a brain cell. Imagine millions of marbles. Heck,

FACT:
The human brain produces many more cells and connections than it could ever use

FACT:
Many brain cells go unused

FACT:
I had a crush on Pam Kingman in the fourth grade

FACT:
The brain starts to prune away the cells it doesn't think it needs.

Wait go back one! Can any computer do what I just did? Spit out rational and extraneous unrelated thoughts whenever it wants. Was it, in fact, unrelated? Probably not. And the subtle connection between brain economy and Pam Kingman probably contains a valuable insight. I could find it if I choose to pursue it. In any case, allowing Pam to hop my train of thought represents a perfect example of a hardwiring escape.

Hardwiring refers to the linear progression of thought processing our brain becomes accustomed to over time. For many kinds of thinking, hardwiring serves us well. But when it comes to creative thinking, hardwiring amounts to self-imposed shackles.

Can we as adults do what I just illustrated or have we become linear thinkers, rote, and pattern-like processors with limiting thinking? Yes, we can break the bonds of linear thinking and, yes, we have become limited. Let's find out how it happened before we learn how to break through our self-imposed limits.

HOW WE GET HARDWIRED

If you obey
all the rules
you miss
all the fun!

– KATHARINE HEPBURN

The brain is so efficient that if, over time, we don't put a part of it to work, that part gets laid off, sometimes forever. Or, to stay with our marbles analogy, we use 'em or lose 'em.

The trillions of connections that survive the great die-off owe their survival in large part to what a child learns in his or her first decade. A highly stimulating early environment can increase the number of connections in a brain by as much as 25 percent or more. But no matter how many connections we collect, we allow them to lull us into thinking patterns. We express these patterns as rules.

Rules help us function in this complex world and we use them to simplify our lives. For example, we don't want to deal with every stop sign we encounter in a new and creative way. It's better to just obey the rule and stop. There are lots of ways to multiply two numbers, but the way we learned in grade school works just fine for most of us. So we'll probably use it for the rest of our lives.

Rules rule, but they come with a trade-off. They tend to make us lazy thinkers. They like us to depend on them and we do. Any rule represents, at best, the latest thinking on a subject. At worst, the last idea standing after some sort of debate, whether or not all sides were considered. For this reason alone, we should question rules and modify them to accommodate our ever-changing world.

All rules can be updated or improved. I know I'm asking for trouble when I apply that statement to religion, politics, race relations, gender differences, and the like. Challenging rules in these areas offends some people personally. And yet you'd be hard-pressed to find a sacred cow—religious, political, scientific—that hasn't tipped a previous cow considered just as sacred.

Nevertheless we find ourselves at the mercy of many senseless rules. Comedians draw a good deal of their material from mocking rules that make little sense. And we laugh, because we realize the silliness of our plight. But we go right back and follow the silliest rules simply because our brains are hardwired and it's so much easier to default to following the rules.

SENSELESS RULES

The groundbreaking, TV program, *Candid Camera*, used hidden cameras to secretly record everyday people at their unguarded best and worst. They often caught folks numbly following senseless rules. One such episode took place in a store with a black-and-white, checkerboard floor. At the entrance a sign read, "Walk on black tiles only." Yes, some customers carefully avoided all the white squares. Another segment captured pedestrians dutifully obeying a sidewalk sign that read, "Backwards Walking Zone."

Candid Camera presented exaggerated examples, but the ordinary cases are more dangerous. We don't need *Candid Camera* to show us how we constantly agree to go along with all sorts of nonsense, sometimes at great expense to ourselves and harm to others.

The entire postmortem industry thrives on our acceptance of useless and expensive customs. Let's face it, we die, we rot. But because we'd rather not confront this fact, especially in our time of sorrow, many bereaved go along with the tradition of burying our loved ones, dressed to the nines, nestled on luxurious cloth, and boxed in rich wood or a top of the line metal.

This morbid glorification of the corpse discourages the very sensible idea of donating vital body and parts. As a result, young and otherwise healthy people die waiting for organs locked deep underground in concrete and steel burial vaults, some advertised as impervious to moisture for 75 years!

Every time you prepare for take off in an airplane, your flight attendant is forced by senseless regulations to show you how to fasten your seatbelt. Okay, we do find first-time fliers on some flights. But the attendants check everybody's belts anyway. And they could easily announce, "If there's anybody who needs assistance with a seatbelt . . . ."

In general, safety notices, on planes and in product instructions, exist to protect the people who provide the service or make the product. Such notices actually pose a danger to the product or service users. After a while, we become immune to safety warnings, because we've learned to ignore so many senseless ones. So when a useful warning does come along, we ignore it, too.

Our eating habits conform to rules we now know make little sense. We eat three meals a day. Based on the way we're built, we'd do better to eat six small meals a day. We'd eat less each time, never stuff ourselves, and give our digestive systems a much easier way to go. And you end up with more energy.

Other rules are just as ridiculous, but not always as harmful, except that they waste time and contradict our objectives. For example, in the United States the non-Christian population (Jews, Muslims, Hindus, Taoist, Buddhists, Wiccans, and other religions, plus agnostics and atheists) amounts to anywhere from 25 to 30 percent of the population. Yet every time someone takes an oath in an American courtroom, they're required to robotically raise their right hand, put their left hand on the Christian Bible and swear. To nearly a third of them, the Christian Bible means nothing. Some of them reject or even resent it. This is going to encourage them to tell the truth?

ACCUMULATE & REGURGITATE

As if it's not bad enough that our brains drive us toward thinking in familiar patterns, we soon meet another enemy of creative, hope-filled thinking while we're still very young and impressionable. That's right, education. Socialization. Aligning with the tribe.

Teachers, victims of hardwiring themselves, run us through a deeply institutionalized process of accumulation and regurgitation. The mission in school, you immediately learn, is to build a library of information given to you by your teachers and the books they assign and give it back the way they want it when they ask for it. (You have to do it in person, because you could easily program a computer to do this kind of thinking for you.)

You're expected to know. You're graded on what you know rather than how you think. If you don't know an answer, it's considered a weakness. You're looked down upon as less than fit in a "survival of the fittest" world.

Just to make sure you understand where you stand, schools line you up behind desks in neat rows. You know you're being measured. You know real success means being the smartest in the room. You can go for it or settle for less. What kid with any spirit wants to be second? Yet, if there are 30 kids in the room, 29 are doomed to come in somewhere from second to worst. Damn, this gets intense!

It gets worse. Your teacher stands at the head of the class, superior to the sum of all the others like you. In order to be recognized, you raise your hand. Your sudden insights and exuberant epiphanies have to wait in line. In order to be heard, you stand and speak. What an effective way to stifle spontaneous enthusiasm. After you speak, the teacher approves or rejects your response.

In short, most of your early ideas—your formative brain connections, your marbles—get filtered and edited by people whose ideas were filtered and edited by people whose ideas were filtered and edited by people whose ideas were filtered and edited . . . and it didn't stop there. Years on the job have taught you to cover your butt, never step up or stand out, give the right answer or keep your mouth shut.

Luckily, along the way, courageous thinkers rebel and force us to reexamine what we think we know. Slowly over time, things change. But, oh, so slowly! You can join the ranks of those who get beyond accumulating and regurgitating. That's part of what this book will do for you. But first we have to get rid of the bad habit that convinces you to put up with it.

TOUGH IT OUT

In the United States, it's the Puritan ethic. In Mexico, they call it *machismo*. In ancient Greece and Rome it was stoicism. You find it all over: the idea that things have to hurt to help. No pain, no gain. Thinking harder makes you smarter. In a nutshell, this fascination with misery is all a bunch of crap.

Worse yet, these masochistic, tough it out philosophies discourage you from extending your reach. They take hard-wiring, solder it down, and make sure it stays that way. You want a better life? Then you want the opposite of toughing it out. Just count the number of inventions inspired by laziness—from the wheel to the computer. You have to conclude that we possess a natural instinct to make life easier not harder.

What kid hasn't cried, *I hate school*? What do we tell them? (Even though we hated school, too.) "Tough it out. Make the best of it. We all have to do some things we don't like." Wait! We're talking to kids here. They're telling us something's wrong. And we tell them to take it!

Kids don't want to sleep in a dark room all by themselves, while mom and dad snuggle. "Be a big kid," we reply. We're told we need to build independence in our children. But we really need interdependence to function properly. Friends and family, co-operation, division of labor, leveraging each other's strengths to build stronger social groups.

Aside from being a backwards philosophy, "toughing it out" speeds up the loss of your marbles. When you force yourself to be satisfied with the way things are you encourage your brain to limit new connection construction. It gets weak in areas like resourcefulness, resilience, and optimism—the very tools you need most to build a better life.

In no time you find yourself faced with a situation or opportunity you're not prepared to take advantage of because you don't have the tools you need. Which reinforces the idea that you just have to tough it out. See another downward spiral coming?

I HATE IT!

Have you ever refused a painkiller because you feared you'd become addicted? Tests clearly demonstrate that pain killers, when used to manage pain, do not addict. Not only is it masochistic to refuse relief, it's bad for you. Pain does damage to your body and mind. It's no different when it comes to holding back your tears, for fear of appearing weak or sentimental. Tears are a kind of pain reliever. They're good for you.

What about what's bad for you? Do you eliminate it or tough it out? When was the last time you wore a suit or pantyhose in blistering heat in deference to a dress code. Or picked up after a teen or spouse rather than make them do it? Did you eat that steak not done to your specifications or send it back?

What do you hate to do? Let's make an "I Hate" list.

√ cutting the grass
√ cleaning the house
√ changing my oil
√ paying bills

Wait, go back! You don't have to change your own oil. Ever. Car dealers, independent garages, quick-service franchises will do it for you. They'll do a better job, properly dispose of your old oil, maybe even notice that your wipers need replacement, and remind you of the next time you need a change. The same goes for every-thing you hate to do. Somebody can do it for you. Some of these services you can afford. Or you can trade services. "I'll do the dishes every night, if you cook. Okay, the dishes and the laundry."

Whatever it takes, if you hate it, get someone else to do it, but use the time you save to improve your life. Use the time you gain to get to those things you've always dreamed of doing. Take up the oboe. Learn to dance. Write poems to a loved one. Create a business plan. Run five miles.

LIFE MAKES YOU NUMB

Well what else would you expect? You're built to revel in pleasure. You seek it. Left to your own devices—no rules, no laws, no responsibilities, and no authorities—you'd wallow in pleasure. Okay, so it's good we give ourselves some limits. But it's one thing to moderate our passions, another to deny them.

As a child, you never had any problem expressing glee, sadness, and anger. When you were mad at your brother you threw a block at him. When the pudding tasted good, you fed some to the dog, the table, or the floor. For the most part, people around you understood you at any given moment. It was evident how and what you felt because you let the world know.

But over time, expression met suppression. Indulgence met sacrifice. You began to keep things within because it took more effort to jump up and click your heels. It became easier to bite your lip than to tell someone straight up how you felt deep down. You do it today. How many times a week do you think you bite your lip rather than express your opinion? Or what marveled you recently that you kept to yourself?

The simple, wonderful gifts of life like the sun peeking through the clouds, the laughter of friends on a street corner, the sweet smells of a spring day—they all become secondary to getting your kids to soccer practice, getting sufficiently prepped for a meeting, or balancing your checkbook. Life made you numb and your will to express yourself went into the crapper.

BACK TO THE MEMO

Let's revisit Dick's memo. I couldn't have asked for a greater endorsement or better substantiation for the outline of this book. Dick's four complaints about me literally fall under each of the four main points of the Think Naked philosophy. (Way to go, Dick.)

I don't like his hair

Like Dick, we all fear whom or what we don't understand. (In Dick's case, he doesn't even understand hair.) Chapter 4, *Wear Your Cape*, attacks fear, the primary inhibitor of naked thinking. It offers ways to create conditions conducive to risk-taking. More importantly, risk-taking without a fear of ridicule such as getting "The Look"—that uncomfortable expression of ridicule people give you when you say something they don't understand. The *Wear Your Cape* chapter is filled with tools and techniques for eliminating fear, creating safe environments, and neutralizing the embarrassment that cripples thinking.

An outsider doesn't know the complexity of our business

(That's the frickin' point, Dick!) Cheating, asking someone who knows nothing about your business is just plain smart. In Chapter 6, Look at Your Neighbor's Paper, I'll ask you to admit that you don't know everything. Second, I'll show you why, in most cases, it's perfectly okay to cheat. Some companies call it benchmarking. In other words, it's okay to get help—smart help, strategic stimulation, sage advice. You'll get a bird's eye view on how and where to look for strategic help in order to better solve any life issue.

Marco Marsan said the word shit in our meeting.

(Yes, Dick, I sometimes express exactly the way I feel. I'll try to keep that kind of shit out my book.) Chapter 7, *Show-N-Tell*, reverses the creativity-choking rules that say, "Wait your turn!" "Speak only when spoken to," and "Raise your hand if you want to go to the bathroom." In this chapter you'll learn how to get in touch with what makes you passionate and to express the amazing exuberance you've suppressed for years in order to create the best life!

THIS PARAGRAPH BELONGS
AT THE TOP OF PAGE #34

> There are no new ideas,
> I've worked in this business for 30
> years and we've tried it all.

(Then why the hell does Dick still draw a salary?) In Chapter 5, *Blockbuster*, I take on the numskull assumption that just because, "That's how we've always done it," we have to keep doing it that way. I'll show you how to systematically destroy conventional thinking, break stereotypes, and challenge authority, the way you did as a child. Not just the rules imposed by authorities, but the ones you impose on yourself. We'll see how changing the rules gets you out of your rut and on with your life.

WHOOPSY DAISY...

THANKS, JANE!

I want to congratulate Jane for her courage. Despite Dick's petty memo, she went around her boss and hired Marco Polo Explorers. We came through for her in a huge way. The moral of this story:

Don't be a DICK.
Be a JANE.

3

SEE SAW

I'm going to use an easy to understand analogy from our childhood. Just because it's cute, don't take it lightly. This is the central point of the book and I want to emphasize its importance. I'm referring to the playground seesaw.

Maybe you called it a teeter-totter. I like to call it a seesaw. Or better yet, for our purposes, *See Saw*. When I write it this way, it delivers both meanings I have in mind and the central idea of this book.

See stands for what and how you see now as an adult—all of it, the sum of your life experience. *Saw* stands for the way you thought as a child—what and how you saw way back when, with your fresh, innocent, efficient, honest eyes.

Any kid knows a seesaw can't work without both sides and that it works better when both sides are balanced. In this obvious observation lies the essence of thinking naked. So let's look at it just a little closer—first, each side of the seesaw, then balance.

SEE

Knowledge
is good.

— EMIL FARBER

What do you *See* today? Responsibilities? Yes. Routine? Yes. Limits? Laws? Schedules? Bills? Taxes? Yes. Yes. Yes.

You've seen a lot. You've taken some hard knocks. You've rolled with some punches and you carry some scars. You've been burned, but you've also learned that fire can heat your home, make a fireplace glow romantically, and turn a couple of raw eggs into a delicious omelet. And that jalapeños can be excruciatingly hot or make that omelet even more interesting.

All of us carry around a world of unique experiences ranging from the tragic to the terrific. It's all useful. You're always learning and you'll keep on learning. Your brain always thinks, whether you want it to or not. It learns without you telling it to. But in order to make the most of how you See, the sum of all your experiences and their importance, you've got to remember they way you Saw as a child.

SAW

> Infancy conforms
> to nobody;
> all conform
> to it.
>
> — RALPH WALDO EMERSON

You *Saw* things much differently when you were a kid on the playground, or at home in your own backyard, bedroom, or playroom. You saw possibilities—more possibilities than limitations.

You saw more possibilities because your life was full of them. There was little to chill your belief that you could achieve all possibilities. Right now. You were already beginning to build your bank of experience, but it was still low in assets. When called upon to solve a serious problem, you had little experience to draw upon. Now that you have a wealth of experience, you find you no longer have the thinking agility you enjoyed as a child.

BALANCE

A child thinks naked normally but doesn't have the life experience to fuel its pure, naked thinking power. Adults have the experience but most have forgotten how to think with the innocence of a child. It's simple, then. Combine the way you Saw things as a child with everything you See as an adult, and you've got one powerful combination. That's the See Saw secret of thinking naked—balancing the sum of your life experience powered by the fresh, vibrant ingeniousness you had as a child.

I assume you have a lifetime of experience—the See side of the equation. My four Think Naked principles will help you rediscover the Saw side and balance your experience with just as much child-like genius. Naturally I'll use kids and the way they think as our primary role models. But I'll also point out exceptional adults who navigate the rough, adult world thinking naked. You know whom I'm talking about. You see them all the time. People who get things done, who walk around with confident smiles enjoying bountiful lives—not in terms of money but bountiful in the number and kinds of choices at their disposal. Now you know what they're up to. They're naked thinkers.

Whether they realize it or not, they're doing what this book prescribes. Okay, no, they probably didn't read this book. Just the opposite. They helped inspire this book. I pepper this book with examples of adults who innately think naked, people who successfully balance their childlike brilliance with their lifetime of adult experience. I still learn from them and I encourage you to as well. By showing you how to think naked, like they do, this book will give you the ability to be as exceptional as the people you admire most.

SEE SAW BALANCE AT WORK

After the Second World War, Alfred Gilman, a biochemist, and Louis Goodman, a physician, set out to find an antidote that would protect soldiers against the horrible effects of mustard gas. Along the way, they noticed that one of the ingredients very efficiently killed lymph cells and white blood cells. Instead of merely listing this effect, they looked at it with kidlike wonder. Looking with kidlike wonder is a Think Naked technique I call "Wow! It's a Cow!" I'll explain it in detail in Chapter 5. Right now I just want to point out the See Saw Balance at work in what Gilman and Goodman did.

Without either the See or Saw side of the balance, the two scientists might not have found an antidote for mustard gas. Thank you very much. But with the combination of their See side (their scientific knowledge and discipline) and the Saw side (their kidlike wonder) they found there was more, they came up with a drug still used to fight leukemia, lymphoma, and some tumors. It's the M in MOPP (Mechlorethamine, Oncovin, Procarbazine, Prednisone), used to fight Hodgkin's disease.

The following chart outlines the See Saw combination in what Gilman and Goodman did. It shows you how they balanced what they could See as adult researchers with what they Saw, that is, using the childlike Think Naked technique called "Wow! It's a Cow!" Most important, it points to the great, unexpected result they achieved.

CHALLENGE	SEE	SAW	RESULT
Find an antidote for mustard gas	Mustard gas efficiently kills lymph cells and white blood cells	Wow! It's a Cow!	Cancer-fighting drug

Although the actual events turned out to be much more complex, I've distilled them to focus on only what we're talking about right now—the balance of See and Saw. You need both to make any progress inventing, discovering, or improving your life in any way.

Because the See Saw Balance is absolutely essential to the Think Naked way of life, I'm going to place See Saw charts wherever I describe a naked thinking breakthrough. Each chart identifies one of the See Saw Balances at work in the breakthrough we examine. There may be more Think Naked techniques at work in each example, but I select one in each case for the purpose of simplicity and clarity. Let the charts remind you that naked thinking is always a combination of what you See with your adult bank of experience and how you Saw life as a four-year-old genius.

In the Think Naked worksheet I've provided at the end of the book, we'll use the same formula, the same balance of See and Saw, to help you meet any challenge you face. If you conscientiously use this formula, your results will be just as exciting.

SOVIET SEE SAW

Let's visit Mikhail Gorbachev, one of my top Think Naked heroes. And what a great example of balance. Imagine the thrill of teeter-tottering the Soviet Union on the seesaw of communism and capitalism. Schooled hard in the rigors of the Communist Party—from his days as a Young Pioneer all the way to his rise to the summit of Soviet power—Gorbachev somehow managed to see through all that he had been taught to See and dramatically revolutionize Russia based on what he Saw, like a child.

As soon as he reached the summit of Soviet power, he introduced two unthinkable reform programs. The first, *perestroika,* set out to restructure the entrenched Soviet system. The second, *glasnost,* called for unprecedented openness. Unheard of! Yet these two naïve notions gave Gorbachev the leverage he needed to reduce military spending, pull the Russian army out of Afghanistan, begin nuclear disarmament, and more.

We all knew he was teetering (or was he tottering?) when he was hit with and survived a coup. By the time he was forced to resign, however, Gorbachev—raised a total communist, limited by what he was taught to See—led his country toward the new and open, democratic horizon he Saw.

WEAR YOUR CAPE

```
                              ☐ URGENT
To _____        A.M.
              Time                 P.M.
Date ___ WHILE YOU WERE OUT
From _____ YOU FORGOT _____
Message _____
_____
_____
          Fear is obvious,
      the way you handle it isn't.
_____
_____
                  — TOMMIE SMITH
Signed _____ 1968 Olympic gold medalist
                          001 Reorder No.
```

This chapter will give you the tools to create an environment conducive to naked thinking. We'll begin by understanding fear itself, the main enemy of your childlike mental agility. Then we'll look at eight easy techniques for quieting fear in yourself and dispelling it in those around you. If you practice all the techniques, you'll be one step closer to a life free of despair.

1. HAPPY PLACE sets the stage for eliminating fear. You'll learn how to create a safe, personal refuge, the way you and I did as kids.

2. **MONSTER UNDER THE BED** shows you how to look your fears in the face.

3. **GO DOWN SWINGING** helps you develop the fear-fighting attitude you need to run with champions.

4. **SANDBOX CITY** lets a couple of kids, unable speak to each other, teach you how to construct an aura of communication with hands, sand, and play.

5. **SUPPORT FIRST** introduces you to a childhood chum who embodies the kind of fear-fighting encouragement you can use to build strong alliances.

6. **FEAR IN YOUR BACK POCKET** shows you how to develop ready, measured responses to all kinds of fear.

7. **GET THE LOOK** equips you to deal with the detractors, who like nothing more than filling you with fear.

8. **DISCOUNT AND REVENGE** gives you a powerful technique for breaking the cycle of fear festering.

I grew up with a kid named John Pferdmenges (Ferd-MENG-gus). He lived next door and always wore a cape—blue with a yellow lightning bolt.

I'd wake up to John yelping as he'd jump off the woodpile. On hot summer nights the last thing we'd see is a streak across the backyard. It was John, arms outstretched, flapping cape in tow. There wasn't anything he wouldn't try. There wasn't anything that seemed to scare him. Was it the cape?

Do you remember having that kind of fearlessness? What made you that way? What could possibly make you that way today? It's a number of things that I'm going to re-introduce you to in this chapter.

POWER TO OVERCOME FEAR

You step alone over the threshold of an old, empty house. Your flashlight beam cuts through the dark, musky foyer, illuminating neglected, dingy walls. An old picture frame displays the cold, hostile face of a stern, scary, old man. You expect to see his ghost any minute.

The floor creaks weakly as you step carefully forward. Something breaks under your foot with a crack that echoes through the house, making the place sound much larger than you imagined. Suddenly a small creature scurries over your foot and down the hallway behind you. Yikes! What else have you disturbed?

"Plink . . . plink" from somewhere below conjures up images of a dank, infested basement. A sudden rush of the room's cold breath chills the back of your head. Fear grips your neck with its hot hand. Your heart pounds. Little beads of sweat rise out of your upper lip. Your breath grows heavy in spite of your efforts to calm it. Tension compresses your chest. You want to scream. You want to run but you can't move.

Alone in the dark, the world can be a horribly frightening place. But in the clear light of day, even a haunted house loses its horror. Let's turn on the lights, open the windows, blow away the dust, clear the air, and chase the scary creatures out of your life. Because, admit it or not, your life is full of fear. Day in, day out, just as in the haunted house, it confronts you.

NAKED THINKING ENEMY NUMBER ONE

Our brains can be both our best friend and our worst enemy. Research shows that when we're in danger, this intricate organ sends out a signal from a part of the brain known as the amygdala. The signal is like a physiological alarm that makes us react to protect ourselves. The feeling we experience during this process, we call fear. Even though the alarm from our amygdala benefits us, the feeling of fear doesn't please us at all. Nature wants it that way. She wants us to avoid danger. She says, "Stove . . . Hot!"

> I've developed a new philosophy. I only dread one day at a time.
>
> — CHARLIE BROWN

Someone comes after you with a knife; your amygdala sends the signal. You drive off a bridge, same signal. A group of friends makes fun of your new piercing—there goes the signal. Someone calls your new idea stupid, same signal. And because it's the same signal, your response to all of these situations feels pretty much the same. So if you don't learn to overcome these sources of fear, you grow numb and incapable of dealing with them.

You can defeat fear. Each of the following *Wear Your Cape* techniques gives you perspective on what a child does automatically and what you can do to combat and win the war over the fear that silences the genius in you and those around you. The way John Pferdmenges used his cape to soar through each day with the fearlessness of a superhero.

WEAR & SHARE

The fearlessness you gain for yourself will come from practicing the first five techniques—Happy Place, Monster Under the Bed, Go Down Swinging, Sandbox City, Fear in Your Back Pocket. Then you'll want to move on. You'll feel so much more confident with your new power over fear that you'll want to share it.

It's only natural. With power comes responsibility. Just as Superman, slowly at first, must have astonished himself with his newfound powers, you'll want everyone around you to be just as fearless as you. The three remaining techniques—Support First, Get the Look plus Discount and Revenge—will show you how to share your fearlessness with your friends, family, coworkers, and anyone you meet.

Like John Pferdmenges and I, Batman and Robin, Superman, Blade, Wonder Woman, and WitchDoctor—like all the superheroes, you'll use your cape to make the world a better place.

HAPPY PLACE

John Pferdmenges created the coolest place under his basement stairs. Maybe it was just a space under the steps, but to us it was a refuge, a place where no one would bother us, especially an adult with some kind of chore. We were invisible and could control the afternoon with the flip of an imaginary switch. Through the spaces between the steps we could fire weapons of mass destruction from the side of our mountain. The handle of his mom's vacuum cleaner was a trap door switch, just in case any bad guys got in. John used crayons to draw a lie detector system with

> We have very few inferior people in the world. We have lots of inferior environments. Try to enrich your environment.
>
> — FRANK LLOYD WRIGHT

a microphone; a complex series of buttons, and two indicators marked *True* and *Fake*. When John would ask you a question, you'd answer into the "microphone," he'd "activate" the machine, and either the *true* or *fake* indicator would "light up." Naturally adults rarely passed the test.

What John and I did was not exceptional. Take a close look at any child who sits alone and plays with a doll or an action figure. Notice how they shut out the rest of the world for as long as they like and create a world of their own. You're watching the power of imagination in its purest, most highly concentrated form. A power you can use to escape fear.

Kids can escape so easily, because we create for them a perfectly protected environment—floor-to-ceiling comfort with Barbie or Batman sheets, cartoon hero posters, and plush dolls. They can play free of serious concerns. And their environment helps distract them from the concerns they may have. Why can't adults do the same?

We adults burden ourselves with tons of concerns. Fear bubbles up out of these concerns as they brew in our brains. To make matters worse, most things around us remind us of pressing responsibilities, possible problems, and potential dangers: the TV news, our appointment books, the pile of bills, the telephone, the mess in the sink. That urge you get from time to time—the one that makes you wish you could just chuck it all and get away—it's telling you, you need a change of scenery.

You knew that. But maybe you didn't know that you don't have to drop what you're doing and abandon everyone and every-thing to get away. You can and should create an environment, a Happy Place, where you feel as secure as you did as a kid. The more suited to you and your likes you make your Happy Place, the more comfortable you will feel in it. The more *true* rather than *fake* you make the space, the better it will serve you.

Your Happy Place doesn't have to be a real place. It can be a state of mind you achieve by doing something you like to do or leaving a situation that causes you grief.

Ever find yourself forced to endure a painfully boring lecture or speech? I mean one that just kills you to sit through. Your eyes start to wander and you notice someone smiling from ear to ear. She's visiting her Happy Place. She may be thinking of her favorite movie star, chocolate, or playing bocce ball this past weekend. That's how easy it can be.

I like to take a long, hot shower. I pay attention to the sounds and sensations, feel the water, breathe deeply, "Ah, Calgon, take me away!" It works wonders. Other people tell me they get the same result from exercising, reading, walking on the beach, or driving in the country. At home you usually can do more to transform your surroundings—turn off the phone, put on your favorite CDs, adjust the shades, fix a pot of herbal tea, or pour yourself a Pepsi Blue. What can you try at work?

When you're having fun—not under pressure to solve your problem or not so fiercely focused on it—you think more creatively and produce more innovative solutions. In your playful, childlike mode, your unconscious mind speaks up. It more readily makes random connections and more easily considers novel solutions. The kind of solutions that can help you overcome fear and defeat desperation.

Unfortunately we're usually too busy to make time for ourselves, let alone retreat to a place for ourselves. We feel too cut off from the world, even guilty, when we go to a personal space. But if you want the benefits of thinking naked, you have to put an end to that kind of self-abuse right now. I mean it! Go to your room!

JOHN STEINBECK'S HAPPY PLACE

The author of *The Grapes of Wrath*, Nobel Laureate John Steinbeck, made his childhood California his Happy Place. According to his son, Thom, "When my father was young, California was a remarkably beautiful place, bursting with lushness. Add his passion for classical themes and you have a perfect setting for his imagination."

California provided many settings for Steinbeck's work. When the market crashed and the Great Depression hit, he moved into a small cottage in Pacific Grove, California. From the Pacific Ocean he took his food as well as his inspiration. He wrote, "Given the sea, a man must be very stupid to starve. That great reservoir of food is always available . . . In the tide pools of the bay, mussels were available and crabs and abalones and that shiny kelp called sea lettuce. With a line and pole, blue cod, perch, sea trout, sculpin could be caught."

Finding your perfect setting is a two-way affair. I think Steinbeck could have created his Happy Place anywhere. As the themes of his work so clearly describe, California life could be miserably wretched. Yet he found human majesty in everything he wrote.

MONSTER UNDER THE BED

Unfortunately no matter how heavenly you make your Happy Place, a little bit of hell always manages to sneak in. What could be happier than the place your parents created for you when you were a child? Your room was a refuge from school, neighborhood dogs, bugs, bullies, bad weather, and whatever else you feared. On top of that, you had a favorite pillow, blanket, or stuffed animal. You arranged your dolls or action figures, you hung posters and pictures. Still, somehow, no matter how wonderful you made your room, fear found a way to invade. All tucked in, safe and snug, you suddenly wondered, "What if there's a monster under my bed?" No sooner than you wondered, the monster became real to your bright and lively imagination.

How did you react to the idea of a monster hiding under your bed? Did you sit up and scream for your parents? Run to your closet, grab a bat, and start swinging at the monster? Or did you bring the bat to your mom or dad and beg them to go after it? All of these reactions are healthy, at least, healthier than cringing beneath the covers drenched in sweat and mortal terror. You made a choice. Your choice brought you more terror or a resolution. It's time to make that choice again.

What do you do today when some threatening fear invades your Happy Place? Do you attack it or cringe? The setting may be different, but the situation remains much the same. And just as in childhood, many of your fears are imaginary or at least exaggerated. Most of them can be eliminated with a simple call for help. Most important, like the monster under your bed, none of them go away all by themselves.

From now on, I want you to handle monsters decisively, with a bat, and someone's help if necessary. Don't accept the ambiguity of whether or not the monster is under your bed. Find out what's making you think it's there. If it's really there, punch it out, jam it in a pillowcase, and toss it out with yesterday's trash.

Let's make it real. Is your boss a jerk? Attack. Let the monster know what makes you uncomfortable. Could this cause another problem? Absolutely. We'll talk about the outcomes you may fear in the next technique, but get this one down first. Here's the point: letting the monster live—under your bed, at home, or on the job—is always worse than confronting it. Failing to assert yourself allows the shadows of fear to shade and eventually darken your life.

I'm going to knight thee. You choose the way you attack the monster, but face the fear! You can attack your monsters several ways. There's the direct method—Sword drawn, face shield down. Your boss, spouse, or friend asks you to do something you don't want to do. You immediately reply, "No. I don't want to." Or "No. I have a problem with that," and explain your concerns. This approach will get results. It's most effective in a place where open communication is encouraged. Most of the time the two of you can easily resolve your differences. But if your boss or spouse is an idiot, there will be some fireworks. Maybe it's time there were.

Then there's the more tactful but still truthful and direct approach—Your sword stays in its sheath, but you've got your battle gear ready. For example, to a boss who makes a troublesome demand, you might reply, "You're the boss. I want my job, but I want to be honest." When you present your concerns this way, you avoid giving the impression that you don't want to cooperate. Use this method when you're dealing with reasonable people who can't handle the direct approach.

Finally there's the pillow fight approach—You start the attack from a flanking position. "You probably didn't mean it, but . . .," or "I must have misunderstood you . . . ." This way, you give the benefit of the doubt but don't leave things unsaid. If this fails, you know you're in a situation you have to exit. Even if that means quitting your job or breaking up a marriage or friendship, you're still much better off having confronted the problem. Now you have a clear course of action.

In each of these approaches, you take an active role in directing your future rather than passively accepting your fate. You confront your monster. In most cases, you won't have to take your principles to the mat. You'll usually find your fear was much greater than the actual threat. Never let fear drown your valuable time and energy. If you fear it, confront it. Fight it if you must, but don't ever let it lurk.

Go Down Swinging

Yes, confronting your monsters means trouble sometimes, but only sometimes. You'll be surprised how often your fears evaporate unfounded, how meekly they slink away sometimes. Most monsters are bullies. Stand up to them and they back down. Some stay away, some come back. But you're always better off finding out what your monsters are made of.

And when they turn out to be real? I hope you're not averse to losing. I hope you don't expect all your confrontations to come out your way. When you get into the habit of confronting formidable fears, you're going to have to get into the habit of winning some and losing some. You might lose most. But again, it's worth it. Here's your choice: Ignore your fears and you always lose. Confront them and you win sometimes. However, winning sometimes, rather than losing all the time, adds up to a winning life.

How often did Pete Rose get a hit for every ten times he came to the plate? Look at his batting average and see the answer—three. That means Pete struck out, grounded out, flied out, or failed to get on base seven out of ten times at bat. And he's the best.

Let's make sure we get this. The greatest hitter in the game lost seven out of every ten confrontations with a pitcher. There was one thing you could bet on, though. When Pete stepped up to the plate, he would go down swinging! The goof would sprint to first base when they walked him. (You're supposed to walk. That's why they call it a walk.)

How many times have you walked away from a situation instead of confronting it all because you feared the outcome? How many times do you avoid a sticky situation rather than risk embarrassment? Where did it get you? Remember Pete Rose next time. If you want to ask someone out, step up and swing. Nail your next job interview. Let the employer know how much you want it. When your next love opportunity, chance to perform, or join a team comes along—give it your best shot.

SANDBOX CITY

Around the time I was six or seven, growing up in Quebec, I'd visit my grandmother, Nonna Anna. She'd take me to the park every now and then, bringing something to keep herself busy, and sit next to an enormous sandbox. There I would play with my shovel, pail, and Matchbox cars. I remember the day a child approached with his mother, sat on the other side of the sandbox, and started to play.

After a couple of minutes of looking up at one another and noticing each other's cool stuff, I walked over and asked if he wanted to use my shovel. He just shrugged his shoulders. I thought it was strange that he didn't answer me. We continued to play, separately. Moments passed. Then he offered a toy to me. When his mother said something to him with words I'd never heard before, I realized he and I had been communicating even though we spoke different languages.

Eventually we started to collaborate. We created a village complete with roadways, bridges, and tunnels. There was a moment when his fingers poked through our first tunnel. We both smiled. We didn't let our language barrier stop us from creating a sandbox city. We had something more powerful—play. Meanwhile our grown-ups never spoke a word to each other.

When a German shepherd meets a French poodle, they have no trouble communicating. They communicate on a more basic level. Aside from the sniffing part, it's just like a couple of kids playing in a sandbox. Children's innocent play looks like fun, pure and simple. Nothing serious going on. Right? Wrong. As they shovel and pour sand, plow imaginary roads, construct and destroy castles, laugh and carry on, kids are teaching each other how to manage the next generation's society. Pretty serious stuff when you think about it, but kids don't think about it, otherwise it wouldn't work.

And that's the point. We all need nonserious interaction with our peers. Let me repeat "nonserious." Getting together just for the heck of it. No agendas. Unlike kids, however, we mistakenly outgrow it. We couldn't be more wrong. An incredible amount of absolutely necessary social weaving happens when we play.

Scientific research shows that social deprivation has severe negative effects on overall cognitive abilities. That's because social interaction develops our thinking abilities. We not only benefit from the ideas of others, we learn a great deal about our own ideas based on how others react to them.

Unfortunately adults tend to rely on themselves and to be wary of others. But children know better. Because they play, they can interact anywhere, with just about anybody, all day long, and into the night. They love to have sleepovers.

Play, more than any other social interaction, reveals what's going on inside your head. Playing with others sharpens your people skills. You get to know people on a deeper, more intimate level. At a sleepover, you even find out who snores, who sleep walks.

The most important part of play is its spontaneity. When we play we goof around, fall down, act silly, and say what comes to mind. But we accept whatever happens. After all, it's just a game. In real life, we set reasonable expectations and get reasonable results. We create comfort zones. We set up rules we hope will protect us from the kind of spontaneity play brings. And the rules work. We end up a lot less spontaneous.

What if you treated your life like a great, big Sandbox City? You can do whatever you want. Make whatever you want to make. Play with whomever you choose. Be whatever you want to be! The best part—you wouldn't have to worry about success. You can't fail. It's your game. With this kind of attitude you'd feel a lot more at ease meeting people and trying out new social adventures.

You'd still be judged by others, but you'd be less stressed about making what other people consider mistakes because they'd be your mistakes. Think about it. How bad is it to make a mistake? You've made billions already. You'll make many more in pursuit of your dream. So what's the diff?

Mistakes you make in pursuit of your dream make you stronger. They teach, so don't let them discourage you. Don't penalize yourself or dock your pay, when you approach a situation with pure intent and integrity. All mistakes are honorable if you make them with pure intent.

FEAR IN YOUR BACK POCKET

The mistake you don't want to make is avoiding a situation that would enlighten and add to your life. That sandbox many years ago and situations since have taught me to distrust the fear and apprehension of a new opportunity. Rather than sitting out and living with not knowing what you missed, get into the sandbox. Make something happen and put Fear in Your Back Pocket.

Putting Fear in Your Back Pocket means predisposing yourself to dealing with the feelings fear generates in a positive way. You're going to face fear sooner or later. What can you do to make the most of it? Fear normally causes us to fight, flee, or sometimes freeze. If you prepare yourself systematically and deliberately, you'll be more likely to make the most advantageous choice and often a surprisingly original choice. That means you have to recognize fear, respond to it, and stay prepared.

The first step is to recognize those moments when fear occurs. This is harder than it sounds, because fear comes in a variety of forms. Some signs are impossible to miss—shortness of breath, pounding heart, the way your surroundings take on an unreal appearance. Others are much more subtle—uncertainty, discomfort, feeling vulnerable or self-conscious, or suffering from lack of confidence. Here are some examples of situations you may or may not recognize as sources of fear or apprehension:

The moment you don't know what to do or what to say. For example, when someone attacks you, makes an aggressive move, or says something very threatening.

Those moments when a script would help, when pregnant pauses occur. For example, when someone makes an unexpected announcement, lowers the boom. When the words "uh" and "err" come all too naturally.

Moments when you just want to avoid human contact. When you prefer anonymity to striking up a conversation or engaging in one.

Moments that create an internal conflict. When you're not sure whether to mind your own business or to do something. You want to avoid taking a stand but realize that doing nothing will compromise your principles.

For these and all kinds of fearful moments, you need to create a number of appropriate, measured responses. We learned in Monster Under the Bed that every fear needs a response. Some you need to attack, while more subtle fears require more subtle engagement. Some monsters you can simply appease with a snack left under the bed.

To see how this works, list some moments like the kind described above. Consider how you might react to each of them. To help you with your list, here are a few moments that have caused me different degrees of fear:

- My best friend dying of Leukemia
- The day my divorce became final
- Coming across a house on fire
- Wishing for a phone call that I knew would never come
- Feeling vulnerable in the face of a relationship

Now what are some of yours? Rehearse the feelings each of these moments gives you in the pit of your stomach. How do you feel? What could you do? What have you done in the past? What did you wish you had done? Which responses would serve you best?

Finally, after you choose the most appropriate responses, rehearse and store them. Put them in your back pocket. Stay prepared, but not in a way that takes up all your time. Just enough to make you feel confident that you can handle just about anything that comes along. Remember, every fear is an opportunity to fix a problem. With this attitude in your back pocket, you will eventually come to welcome challenging situations that may have paralyzed you in the past.

Now that you know how to put Fear in Your Back Pocket, you're ready to help the rest of your world conquer their fear.

MANAGING FAILURE

There was a manager who made a series of decisions that lost his company a ton of money. He assumed his boss, Mr. Watson, would fire him. But after hearing the manager's side of the story Mr. Watson said, "We can't fire you, we've invested too much in your education."

Wouldn't it be great if all bosses were like Mr. Watson? The best bosses are. They discourage laziness and carelessness, but they also encourage experimentation and risk-taking. Because there's nothing wrong with honest mistakes, unless you keep making the same mistakes over and over again.

You can make the most of mistakes by learning what not to do again. Scientists look at mistakes as steps on the way to discover, the most valuable part of the process of elimination, identifying the dead ends.

Never regret mistakes. Just don't forget to look for the unexpected wonders mistakes are famous for creating. Like Ivory Soap. As the legend goes, someone left a batch of ingredients cooking a little too long and the soap came out full of air. We don't know if the cooks were fired or not, but the company, Procter & Gamble, sent the botched soap home with their employees. Soon word got back to the top brass that everyone loved the "soap that floats!" You know the rest.

And let's not forget that discovering America was an accident. For what he set out to do, find a route to the far east, Columbus might be considered a failure. But he certainly made the most of what he encountered. No discovery is a failure, unless we have our minds made up about what we are going to find. So if your mind isn't made up about Columbus, applaud your own spirit of discovery.

Always make the most of whatever happens. And don't just let things happen. Make things happen!

SUPPORT FIRST

Lori Smiler flew through the air, faster than any of us boys. In running races, she'd kill us. Same age. Lori was just incredible. When she'd beat us, though, she'd never rub it in. Lori always supported first. And we, naturally, always wanted Lori on our team.

I don't know if Lori understood the idea of Support First, but how hard is it to understand? It's simply a matter of giving someone something we all crave. And it's not chocolate. Kids need it so they don't regress into a shell. Adults need it to find their full potential. Lori gave it and made us her loyal friends. I'm talking about praise, plus something more—a habit of giving praise before you do anything else.

Support First! For anything that's served up. When you respect a child in their sometimes awkward and painful efforts to discover themselves, it gives them the confidence they need to grow into a well-adjusted child. This goes for everyone from your coworkers to your spouse. When you support first, you're more likely to build confidence in the person you support. When you put someone on the defensive, you get the opposite effect. Supporting before you do anything else benefits everyone involved.

Here's an example on how to use it. When someone volunteers a thought, any thought, condition yourself to support them first. They are revealing their soul in some way, so don't step on it, you twit! Help build on their thought. Don't be shocked, even if they serve up something unexpected. All truly novel thinking seems a little ridiculous at first. Hear them out. Build on their thoughts. Help their idea live. Besides, it makes sense to see if an idea bears fruit before chopping down the tree. The most important creative resource children and adults have is encouragement in whatever they do.

EXERCISE
Say You Like It

What do you do when someone you live or work with screws up? In short, condition yourself to resist giving automatic criticism. More specifically, take the following simple steps next time, and I promise you, everyone will come out a winner.

LISTEN. Resist your urge to judge, and consider what really happened. When you get all the facts, all sides of the story, things might be better than they seemed at first.

LIKE. Say you like it. Find something in the mistake you can use to encourage the people you assume have just busted their butts for you.

LEARN. Extract a lesson from the loss. Make sure everyone understands what was learned. In fact, it's best to draw the learning out of them rather than dictating it to them.

If you practice these three steps—listen, like, learn—you'll get a whole lot more cooperation and better results all around.

PROFUSE PRAISE

You can take Support First to an even higher level. I used to tell my son, Shane, "I love you," a hundred times a day. (In fact I still do.) I used to kiss him fifty times a day. Now I have to sneak kisses in. (He's bigger than I am.) I was always struck by his willingness to receive my hugs and kisses. Here I am, a big guy giving smooches to my man-child son, whenever and wherever, and he'd always oblige. Every now and then I'd ask him, "Does Dad kiss you too much?" He'd always reply, "Nah!" with a tone as if to say he didn't want to break my heart by saying, "Dad, enough with the kisses already."

Profuse Praise works very much the same way. We may at times say, "Thanks, enough already," but the truth is, you can't praise someone enough. Not the gratuitous, disingenuous praise with that award show feel. I'm talking about telling a coworker, spouse, or child how much you appreciate them whenever you feel it. Look around you right this second. Is there someone within earshot of a compliment? Think it through, load it up, and deliver some profuse praise. If nothing else, you'll get to watch them smile or look at you funny.

GET THE LOOK

Great spirits have always found
violent opposition from mediocrities.
The latter cannot understand it
when a man does not thoughtlessly
submit to hereditary prejudices but
honestly and courageously
uses his intelligence.

— ALBERT EINSTEIN

Have you ever said something in a room full of people and received "The Look?" You propose what you think is a great idea or thought, and faces contort. They look puzzled, even disgusted. You feel a flush in your face. Your heart races. The chances that you'll volunteer another thought become nil. But wait, "The Look" doesn't always mean what you think. When people struggle to understand something, the struggle also shows on their face.

How you read "The Look"—as an insult or as support—is up to you. You can imagine the negative, "I think you found the instructions, pal, but you weren't supposed to smoke them! Yuk! Yuk!" Or the positive, "Wow! I never heard anything like that before. Tell me more while I try to wrap my feeble mind around your visionary thought." Whenever you get "The Look", especially when you are part of creating a novel solution to a problem, it probably means you've proposed something truly original. In this case, "The Look" is more like a thumbs-up. It depends on how you interpret it.

You can even perceive support from the worst kind of detractors. Let's pretend someone gives you "The Look" in order to make you feel stupid—the kind of look that really intends to condemn your exuberance. Don't get on the defensive. No, just the opposite. Help this person immediately. They may have developed a serious medical condition, which causes them to evaluate a thought before that idea has had a chance to take hold or develop roots. This condition is quite serious, quite debilitating. The subject may be suffering from *premature evaluation*. Get them immediate attention, show them that with some training they can rid themselves of this condition and enjoy themselves and life a bit more!

The secret of Getting the Look—is learning to forgive the boneheaded shortcomings of premature evaluators.

DISCOUNT & REVENGE

Almost every day, my brother Richard and I would run into our nemesis, Jimmy Tebo. He lived three doors down the street. This little dude had the sharpest flattop. Literally, sharp points of hair sticking up all over. It made him look like an electrocuted Elvis. Excellent haircut for a nemesis!

Jimmy and a few of his friends got into a mudball fight with Richard and me. It all ended when Richard led us in a charge on their fort—Jimmy's backyard picnic table turned on its side. We were sure they had run out of ammo and were busy making more. Wrong. We ran dead into a fusillade of mud. My brother got it right between the eyes. He looked like Cyclops standing there stunned. Then he dropped to his knees. We all ran to him make sure he was okay.

Jimmy Tebo and I walked him to the water faucet on the side of the house. It was just like you see in the movies when a wounded soldier walks between two of his buddies. Richard's arms were across our shoulders, our arms around his waist. Somehow he had also developed a limp. We showered him with encouragement, "You're gonna make it, Richard. We're almost there. Hang on, man!"

As my brother washed his face, both Jimmy, his enemy, and I, his brother, loaded him up with praise for risking it all. "Nice try, Richard," I told him. "Yeah," Jimmy added, "If you hadn't got hit, you guys would've smeared us." That's the way every conflict ended. No matter who won, at the end of the day we'd all shake hands and make our plans for tomorrow. That's why Jimmy Tebo loved being our nemesis. (I think we called him our archrival.) And no matter how devious his attacks, we loved taking him on. Wouldn't it be great if adults could forgive so easily?

What's the typical adult reaction? Someone "disses" you, you diss them back. Somebody hits you on the forehead with a mudball . . . Well, you get the picture. The ability to apologize and get over it, to break the cycle of insult—somewhere along the line, we lost it. Instead we choose to live with the lingering threat of reprisal. Our unforgiven wrongs fill us with lingering fear. Allowing ourselves to take part in the cycle perpetuates the fear.

Woven into an effective cape must be the healthy reconciliation process that children do so much better than adults. Adults need to be right. It seems we can't get over a slight or an insult without an apology or making someone pay. For kids it's not about being right, it's about getting back to the important stuff—having fun. If you have to apologize to get there, regardless of who's at fault, then so be it. Why stay mad when you've got a snowman to build? What a waste of energy! Rise above the fray; direct your efforts towards construction. This skill will freak out your tough, vengeful adult nemeses, they'll end up standing there, mud balls in hand with no one to fight.

It's going to happen to you today. Someone will say something to you in a condescending way—at the dry cleaner, at work, on a date. When they discount you, tell them about the technique of Discount and Revenge. Tell them that even though you've been discounted, you're not going to exact revenge. Be first, the one who breaks the cycle, the one with the power to break the cycle of discount and revenge. Chances are you'll get "The Look".

FORGIVENESS TEST

History taught us to forgive some people after an initial public mistake or failure. How forgiving are you? Give yourself three points for each time you forgive.

- John Travolta for being a sweathog

- Bruce "Born in the USA" Springsteen for going buff

- Danny "Partridge" Bonaduce for irrepressible cuteness

- Joe Camel for not admitting what that bump on his back was really from

- Ricky Schroder for SILVER SPOONS

- Steven Spielberg for 1941

- Vanessa Williams for posing in PLAYBOY

- Ford for the Edsel

- Coca-Cola for New Coke

- President George Bush, the elder, for puking on Japan's Prime Minister

- Michael Jordan as a baseball player

How many stars did you earn? This was not a real test, just me having some fun. Forgive me! But it does have a point. If you can forgive some of these knuckleheads, what's holding you back from forgiving those a lot closer to you? So who are they? Who do you need to forgive? Make a list and see how well you do.

Let's assume you've read and understand all eight techniques in this chapter. You've begun to put them into practice. How will you know they're working? It's simple. When things that frightened you in the past no longer hold their horror. The following exercise will help you see how you're doing.

EXERCISE
Fears Checklist

Make a list of whatever frightens you. Start with the most frightening. As you practice the Wear Your Cape techniques, you'll notice that some of them no longer frighten you. Cross off your fears as you conquer them. Some fears will take longer to conquer than others. But by practicing the techniques and keeping track of your progress, you'll eventually conquer all of them.

Here are a few common fears. Use them to help build your own list.

- Speaking in public
- Confronting issues with your spouse, boss, children
- Asking someone for a date
- Heights, the dark, crowds, spiders
- Going to the doctor or dentist

Naturally there will always be times when things frighten you. But now you have your cape—the foundation for dealing with fear. The following chapters will give you techniques for developing naked thinking skills. You can't use them effectively when you're mired in fear. So make sure you're wearing your cape before you go any further.

With a working cape on your back, you're ready to jump into the tub and cleanse yourself of how you currently think. You are able to wash away all the conventional thinking habits you've accumulated while growing up. *Blockbuster* will help you realize that the way you think can make or break your chances of leading a life full of optimism, opportunity, and success. Meanwhile, wear your cape. Feel the power. Attack the fear.

BLOCKBUSTER

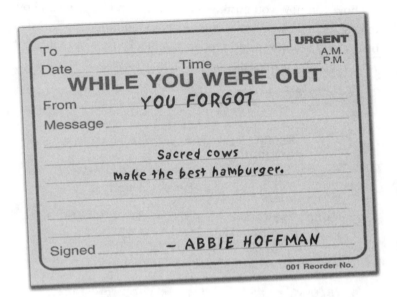

To _____ ☐ **URGENT**
A.M.
Date _____ Time _____ P.M.
WHILE YOU WERE OUT
From _____ *YOU FORGOT* _____
Message _____

Sacred cows
make the best hamburger.

Signed _____ — ABBIE HOFFMAN

001 Reorder No.

Okay, raise your hand if you thought of the folks who rent movies when you saw the chapter title. Hands down, please. Now, a show of hands from those who thought of, *Star Wars, Titanic,* or another movie that broke attendance records.

Ha! Gotcha!

Who pictured a child happily destroying a stack of building blocks? A just built, neatly stacked, four-foot high feat of architectural genius. *Bam!* Ready to start over again. That's the kind of blockbusting I'm talking about. But the fact that you thought of the other kind demonstrates the first point of the chapter. Your brain is hardwired.

In this chapter I'm going to take you back to your childhood to show you how you busted blocks and then I'll show you how to bust mental blocks today. We'll examine common blocks, listed below, and see how its accompanying Blockbuster can replace it with a new, more versatile, optimistic, naked way of thinking.

BLOCK: Been There, Done That
BLOCKBUSTER: Wow! It's A Cow!
Shows you how to uncover a world
of ideas in everyday things

BLOCK: That's the Way We've Always Done It
BLOCKBUSTER: Freshness Dating
Gives you a way to keep
your inventory of ideas fresh

BLOCK: Keep Your Nose To The Grindstone
BLOCKBUSTER: Space Out
Destroys the myth that you
have to drill down to find answers

BLOCK: It's All About Me
BLOCKBUSTER: A Day in the Life
Shows you how to find opportunity
by walking in someone else's shoes

BLOCK: Don't Mess With Success
BLOCKBUSTER: If It Ain't Broke, Break It
Counters the assumption that
if something's working, it's working right

BLOCK: Everything's Copasetic
BLOCKBUSTER: Brain Wedgies
Gets you out of your comfort zone
and into the growing experience

Remember the *You Lost Your Marbles* chapter? We learned that your brain likes to slip into a rut. So much so that smart companies can predict how your brain will respond to their messages. They know if they beat something into your head a certain number of times, you'll think of them when making a purchase. Pretty scary!

A company like Blockbuster spends a lot of time and money trying to make you think of them when you see or hear the word *Blockbuster*. They want that word, their blue-ticket logo, and eventually the very idea of renting movies to be branded on your brain. And they know they can do it, because of the way your brain works—because of its tendency to hardwire.

You've already learned that your brain is composed of billions of neurons connected to each other every which way—that the connection-making process started before you were born. That it never really ends, but as you get older many of these connections tend to become permanent, and the more permanent the connections, the more predictable your behavior. The more predictable your behavior, the more likely you will act, react, and handle situations the same old way.

HAPPY HUMBUG

Patterns are difficult to break, but breaking them is so refreshing!

What kinds of things just happen in your life? On Friday night, Halloween, New Year's Eve, your birthday? What do you do every Christmas? What could you change?

Things take on greater importance or significance when you change them. That's how habits and customs get their importance. "Instead of going to the movies like we do every Saturday night, let's rent a bunch, make some popcorn, and stay home." A new tradition starts. And it stays until you break that pattern and try something new.

Let the record show that every tradition appeared first as something to do instead of nothing or instead of an already established tradition. The big one, Christmas, knocked over a variety of winter solstice celebrations. And it continued to evolve. The Christmas we call a "dyed-in-the-wool" tradition today is a product of Victorian England. And it's still evolving.

Funny thing about traditions, follow them mindlessly and they lose their meaning. Put them to the test by breaking their patterns and they come up with more meaning. That's the beauty of block-busting or any kind of pattern breaking.

What do you take for granted? What habits, daily patterns, holiday, or traditions do you do without thinking, without gaining any real satisfaction? Write them down. Then take some time to consider what you could change about each one. For example: spending Christmas on the beach, giving your friends presents on your birthday, getting up a little earlier and taking the long way to work, or brushing your teeth with your other hand.

I guarantee you'll surprise yourself with every pattern you break. And the patterns you return to, you'll appreciate all the more after having put them to the test.

> Common Sense is the collection of prejudices acquired by age eighteen.
>
> —ALBERT EINSTEIN

Think of your brain as an electronic circuit—that is, the arrangement of wires in any electric device. Radios, toasters, airplanes, factories, and your house all contain circuits. Electric power zips from one point to another through these circuits. Most circuits are hardwired. That means their wires and parts are soldered, crimped, screwed down—permanently connected, so that when you flip a switch or press a button, something happens, usually the way you expect it to happen.

There's no need for you to bother the circuit in your toaster. Just drop in your Pop-Tart and push the lever. Electricity flows from the power plant in your town to your home, through your toaster and its heating element to toast your tasty treat. Just the way you want it.

Your brain can work the same way. I write "Blockbuster" and you think of the movie renters. Your brain has been hardwired to make that association. It's hardwired in a lot of other ways, too. Language is hardwired. When you talk to your friends, you don't have to think about what their words mean. Hardwiring serves us well.

But when it comes to imagining better ways to do things—composing songs, writing an essay, outsmarting an opponent, attracting a mate, baking a better pie, catching more fish, making more money, finding a new job, launching a new career—hardwiring gets in the way. To appreciate and capture new opportunities, you have to break out your thinking rut. You have to snip your hardwiring. Like a kid building a block tower, you have to become a Blockbuster and break the old circuitry.

I have no doubt that you, like most kids, piled your blocks up and knocked them down again and again. You might have done the same with sand castles at the beach. Maybe you raked fallen leaves into great piles, then jumped and rolled around in them, or dressed your Barbie doll for the prom, only to change outfits five minutes later. Or did you build a snow fort and demolish it in an all-neighborhood snowball war? As a naked thinking kid you naturally enjoyed the process of destroying the things you created.

But even as a kid you also began to feel the need to hardwire. For example, you pointed to a car, said "car," and your parents praised you. Then you met a kid your own age and showed off your new knowledge. Your new friend was just as thrilled as you to share the word *car*. But then you pointed to a truck and said "car" again. Your friend corrected you. Sure enough, when you checked with the ultimate authority, your parents, you learned that your friend was right.

Not everything that moves noisily and quickly down the street was a car. The big ones were trucks. This called for mental rewiring. You destroyed your idea of "car," recreated a more refined idea, and added the idea of "truck." Inside your brain, even though you couldn't feel it, new connections formed and some of the original connections were blown. You rewired your brain.

Your childhood was a festival of wiring and rewiring. Of making, breaking, and remaking connections. This process peaked around age four or five and continued, gradually slowing, through your teens. Meanwhile neurons that couldn't find a job got mothballed. We used to think these idle neurons were fired forever, but we've learned that they were just laid off and could be called back to work, but not without some effort. By the time you reached adulthood, most of your brain settled for the connections already wired there.

As an adult, you operate to a great degree at the mercy of the connections made in your childhood. Big events, especially painful experiences can alter your hardwiring. A messy break up can rewire your brain enough to make you more cautious and responsible about dating. Working with someone who cheats the system can either make you a cheater or make you distrust everyone you work with. But for the most part, with a few exceptions, most of your hardwiring happened early in your life.

SISTER POWER

For more than 15 years scientists have been studying a group of nuns in Mankato, Minnesota. The nuns of Mankato live longer than most women, but more important, their lives are teaching us some new lessons about how to stay mentally healthy longer.

David Snowdon of the University of Kentucky leads the Nun Study. He has determined that genes, strokes, diet, intelligence, education, emotion, and other factors all have an effect on mental health in old age. Some of these things we can control. For example, if you exercise your brain throughout your life, you just may extend its life. The evidence—nuns who taught school during their careers ended up with better mental health than those who had less mentally challenging careers.

It just makes sense that continuously exercising your brain keeps your neurons alive and thriving. The Nun Study now supports that notion, and the notion that it's never too late. These intellectually active women write meditations and letters to their representatives. They work all sorts of puzzles and brainteasers. Their lives are mentally challenging. And the ones, who rise to the challenge, keep their brains as healthy as possible. They suffer less dementia in old age, even among those predisposed to Alzheimer's disease.

There's no need to eliminate hardwiring, you just need to know how to get around it, because there's no future in letting yourself become totally hardwired. Your brain does a pretty good job as a hardwired computer, but nowhere near as fast or as accurately. What your brain does in milliseconds seems like eons to a computer. Even though chess master Gary Kasparov can give IBM's Big Blue something to think about, he's no match. It's easy to see, the brighter future lies not in thinking like a computer but in imagining new and better possibilities all the time.

> Computers are useless. They can only give you answers.
> — PICASSO

And that's just what you can do, because your brain's connections are much more flexible than a computer's. Your computer will always read "4" when you input "2 + 2." But your brain can come up with "5" or any other number plus creative reasons why. In fact, there would be no such thing as numbers if we humans hadn't invented them. We can make them do whatever we want. They can even do voodoo. Remember Reaganomics?

The problem is, even though your brain can think out of the box, like 2 + 2 = 5, it defaults to thinking like a computer. Its natural tendency is to become and stay hardwired, for good reason. You no longer have to think how to hold a knife and fork, write your name, and blow your nose. These skills are pretty well hardwired into your brain. It doesn't mean you can't rewire them. You don't want to. You've got better things to do. The same goes for more sophisticated skills you learned later in life—riding a bicycle, playing the piano, swinging a golf club or a tennis racket, and so on.

Unfortunately, repetition and habits can make everything hardwired—what you think of yourself, the limitations you think you've reached, what you can and can't do because of your gender, race, religion, nationality, or sexual orientation. Your job title might limit you in your own mind. Corporate policy, political jargon, conventional wisdom, and your boss's negative performance review all run the risk of becoming hardwired.

The job of this chapter is to help you understand what has happened to you very quietly and gradually over the years and to help you undo this hardwiring at will. In order to do that, you're going to have to break some tried and true thinking habits. You've got to learn how to become a blockbuster. Becoming a Blockbuster will make your life better—guaranteed. But more than that, you'll feel the benefits daily because the little issues will become irrelevant. Now more than ever before, all of us deal with more and more rapid change than at any other time in history. Change and hardwiring don't get along too well. Change demands new solutions. Hardwiring produces the same ol', same ol'.

It's simple, then. The changing world requires you to break free of your hardwiring. To do some serious blockbusting like you did as a kid. It's not only the only way to deal with change; it's the perfect way. Being a Blockbuster doesn't mean becoming an anarchist and destroying everything you've ever learned. It means embracing the belief that there's always more, always a better way, and mustering the courage to knock down some of your blocks in order to find a better way.

When you rely on your hardwiring, you're banking on your best thinking to date. Call it conventional wisdom, which is just fine for solving conventional problems. But when the ground rules change, as they do every day, the best thinking comes up short. On the other hand, blockbusting opens your mind to all sorts of possibilities.

And that brings you to a choice. Door #1: Stay satisfied with your brain hardwired the way it is. Or, Door #2: Get ready to do some strategic blockbusting. Behind the hardwired door, you'll find just what you expect—more of the same. Behind the blockbusting door, a world of possibilities and the chance to become more cerebrally nimble. What's your choice?

Door #2 right? You've made the right choice. Now we're ready to learn and use the following blockbusters. Each one includes at least one exercise that will help you put theory into practice. Don't hesitate to do the exercises. They'll really help you and they're not difficult. Remember this, four-year-olds are natural Blockbusters. They do it without thinking twice. So it's not like I'm asking you to do something you haven't done before.

BLOCK: Been There, Done That
BLOCKBUSTER: Wow! It's A Cow!

Look at this picture:

It's a cow. So what, it's a cow.

We dismiss thoughts quickly because we've become a sound-bite society, too busy to look, too busy to be disturbed. We've become quick at categorizing most of what we see. When we see a cow, we think, "cow." Thank you very much. We don't usually think beyond the obvious.

As a kid, remember, you were fascinated by anything new. You weren't interested in getting to the simplest connection. You were making as many connections as possible. Most of what you saw was new, a first. So, of course, a cow was cool, even though it seems ordinary now.

Today as an adult you have to do a little work to really be impressed with a cow. You have to look twice. Maybe three times. But more important, you have to expect more. In order to expect more, it helps if you develop the attitude that everything is cool.

Are Ella Fitzgerald and Miles Davis cool? Of course. That was too easy, but what about an ant? It carries 400 times its weight. An aardvark? Look at that tongue! Aerial photos of your house, the chlorophyll in grass. What else is cool? What about a cow? It's like a portable dairy. Look for the cool in anything, and you'll find it.

I promised we'd return to how Gilman and Goodman used "Wow! It's a cow!" to come up with a cancer-fighting drug. Let's refer to the See Saw chart again.

CHALLENGE	SEE	SAW	RESULT
Find an antidote for mustard gas	Mustard gas efficiently kills lymph cells and white blood cells	Wow! It's a Cow!	Cancer-fighting drug

In order to get from *See* to *Result,* Gilman and Goodman might have gone through something like, "Wow! This stuff kills all kinds of fast-growing cells. Wait a minute. Wildly fast-growing cells cause Cancer. Wow! Let's see if this stuff kills cancer cells!" Okay, maybe they didn't say "Wow!" every step of the way, but you get the idea. Now you can apply this same kind of concentrated amazement to discover ways to improve your life.

Here are two practical exercises for developing a "Wow! It's a cow!" attitude. They'll help you remove your boredom filter. Each one challenges you to look at something as ordinary as a cow and ignore your first, automatic, hardwired reaction. It will also help if you pretend you've never seen the thing before. Then, to look again and really see it for the first time.

EXERCISE
Ask Who, What, Where,
When, Why, and How?

Look at an everyday object like a floppy disc. Why does it have a square hole in one corner? Why is another corner shaved off? What makes the metal slide snap back into place? Where does all the data go? How much smaller could it be? How much more data could it hold? When are they going to make edible floppies? Do they already? Why do we call them floppies?

Asking questions rather than making assumptions brings you back to your childlike way of thinking. Questions spark your curiosity and ignite your imagination. Adults think they have the answers. "That's a floppy disc, kid." The kid instantly wants to know why it doesn't flop.

EXERCISE
Say "Wow!" Three Times

After you're comfortable with questioning, you'll find you can make richer observations more easily. Look at another everyday object and say "Wow!" Follow it with an observation—something you haven't noticed before. Repeat as often as it takes to uncover a useful, new idea.

Traffic Light

- "Wow! That traffic light looks like a decoration."

- "Wow! I could hang a traffic light in my office."

- "Wow! It could let people know whether or not I want to see anybody."

Make this the way you think, allow yourself to contemplate a flower, to look under a carpet to see how it's bound. Soak in as much as possible. No input is useless. Learning the names of the Jackson 5 may seem inconsequential until you find yourself naming your first son "Tito."

"WOW! IT'S VELCRO!"

How many times have you walked out of the woods with burrs stuck to your socks, pants, even your dog? Swiss engineer George de Mestral encountered the same annoying problem back in 1948. Unlike most of us who simply remove the burrs, George asked a couple of "Wow! It's a Cow!" questions. "Why do cockleburs stick to cloth and hair? How do they do it?" Next he made a couple of "Wow! It's a Cow!" observations. "These little buggers really stick. Maybe I could do whatever they do to make a new kind of fastener." Then he examined a cocklebur under a microscope and invented Velcro.

Notice the difference between George and the rest of us. Instead of merely getting annoyed with burrs, he wowed over their fastening power. He saw possibilities. He busted the blocks that would have made him settle for the typical hardwired reaction.

When you add "Wow! It's a Cow!" questions and observations to your daily life, you too, will discover surprising solutions for the problems you're working on.

CHALLENGE	SEE	SAW	RESULT
Remove cockleburs	Microscopic hooks	Wow! It's a Cow!	Velcro

THE BRAIN CHAIN REACTION

Let's examine what happens in your brain when you have an idea. Basically your idea is nothing more than an electrical impulse transmitted by the neurons in your brain. You can experience it, evaluate it, express it, follow it back to its origin, or just let it take you wherever it goes.

If you let it go, it will spark another impulse that will spark a third and a fourth. In fact, your idea can set off a chain reaction of impulses that will light up your brain like a switchboard. Some people call this daydreaming. I call it a Brain Chain Reaction. It sounds powerful. It is. A Brain Chain Reaction in your brain can stimulate one in somebody else's brain. A room full of people brain chaining . . . Well, you get the idea.

In order to brain chain, you need to develop your brain chain reflex. To do this, think of any idea as a means to an end rather than the end. One idea rarely gets you where you're going. So create a chain of ideas and follow it. Think of every small idea as a steppingstone along the path to an incredible solution. Eventually you'll get used to letting your mind wander. You'll develop the brain chain reflex.

Once you learn how to engage your brain chain reflex you can develop new thoughts and ideas by linking them to one another in a process called brain chaining.

How to start a brain chain

Brain chains sometimes start with a rough idea or a gut reaction to a problem. "Damn these cockleburs!" Sometimes they start with a simple, straightforward question. "What would it be like to ride on a beam of light?"

As ideas start springing up, you need to consider each one at face value. Play with it. Noodle it. Reverse it, invert it, expand and contract it, wander with it. Give it some room to breathe and expand. Follow your instincts and inclinations. Let random thoughts and suggestions stimulate you.

Don't throw anything away. Record every idea. Draw a link (a line) to the idea it came from. Make links to any other ideas the new idea relates to. Draw pictures, doodle, and use a variety of colored pens. Make your brain chain bold and colorful.

When you brain chain with others, remember Support First from *Wear Your Cape*. Build on other people's ideas. Don't evaluate any idea until you're finished brain chaining. Don't even think of any idea as good or bad. Instead, look at each idea, as it is—a step to a bigger and better idea. Spend some time with each idea. Get to know it. Understand its potential. Imagine where it could take you.

How does a brain chain work?

I knew you'd ask that question. You're starting to practice "Wow! It's a Cow!"

Ever say, "I'm going to think this thing through?" A brain chain is a visual representation of you thinking something through. It charts your brain's idea processing. The result looks like a corporate organization chart, with circles strung together with little lines. Below you can see an actual brain chain for a Marco Polo Explorers client:

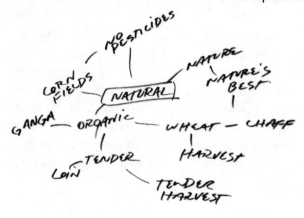

New to the world ideas rarely come fully formed in a single bolt from the blue. They happen with round after round of refining and recombining ideas. Brain chain reactions are made up of lots of smaller ideas. Computers. The telephone. Pampers diapers.

James Burke wrote a book, starred in a PBS series, and writes a monthly column in *Scientific American* all about the connections that lead, like a brain chain, from idea to idea to civilization's greatest breakthroughs. (Clever little dude even named the book, the show, and the column *Connections*.) You could say Burke's work is one big brain chain—his career, an ongoing brain chain.

LAZY THINKERS

> Genius is
> one percent
> inspiration and
> ninety-nine percent
> perspiration.
>
> – THOMAS EDISON

Most people complain that they aren't creative thinkers. That's because they're lazy thinkers. They get ideas all right, but they stop after their first or second Brain Chain Reaction. Thinking is hard work. If it were easy, everybody would be Einstein and nobody would take out the garbage. All the barbers would be unemployed. *Playboy* subscriptions would drop by half. Hugh Heffner would be forced into something like farming. He'd raise the world's biggest tomatoes. Sliced bread and lunchmeat would have to match. Refrigerators would take up most of the kitchen. Eventually they'd become the kitchen. People would live in their refrigerated kitchens. The lighting inside them would be cost-prohibitive. And we'd all be lost in a dark, cold world.

BLOCK: *That's the Way We've Always Done It*
Blockbuster: *Freshness Dating*

It seems that every day scientists learn more about how our brains capture and retrieve information, ideas, and memories. They no longer believe that the brain actually stores them the way we store goods in a warehouse. All the same, brain content might as well take up space. That is, it's difficult to hold information that contradicts other information. So we can still use the warehouse analogy.

If we think of our brains as well organized warehouses, we can imagine that children have a lot of room to fill. They tend to be more curious, asking about everything they see. What is it? How does it work? Why? They're open to our answers just as if they had plenty of room in their warehouses.

When we adults have questions, we look first for answers in our warehouse of stored information. Unfortunately, in our rapidly changing world, a lot of stored information turns out to be pretty stale. What is house music? Is it cool to say, "I'm down with that?" Does that mean I'm groovy, a dope, or just a dork who's trying too hard.

We can go to the grocery store for a solution to staleness—freshness dating. Whenever you're called upon to cough up information, check the date. Make sure you're not regurgitating old, stinky, hard-wired data. But don't stop there. Keep stocking your shelves with fresh produce. It may contradict some of the moldy info you've held on to but that's good. It's time to pitch it.

EXERCISE
Bring Yourself Up-To-Date

Don't sit there satisfied with the most popular network news show. Catch them when you can, but dig deeper. Follow at least one current news story in greater detail than most of your friends. Stay on top of all the facts. Take an avid interest in a popular trend. Keep up with several serious fields, in addition to the one that pays your rent. Get fanatical about a sport, some kind of music, fashion, or one of the fine arts.

EXERCISE
Get Esoteric

Absorb yourself in something few other people follow. Like origami, antique bottle caps, UFOs, ancient Mesopotamian accounting principles, Canadian minor league broom hockey, fancy satin mice varieties, your family tree, Chinese philosophers, taxidermy, worm farming . . . something that tweaks your imagination.

EXERCISE
Ponder Nonsense

Nonsense stretches your brain. It's also fun. It helps you think about things that don't exist or can't be. So how can we talk about them? Read Alice's *Adventures in Wonderland*. Ponder the following two self-contradicting statements.

There are only two groups of people in the world: those who fall into one of those two groups and those who don't.

Everything I say is true, except what I just said.

Ponder the imponderables. Try to answer in your own way, the world's ultimate questions. These questions may or may not ever be answered. But thinking about them will lead you to some interesting ideas. It will also clear out some of the cobwebs in your warehouse.

- Why is there something rather than nothing?

- Does Nameless Creek in Indiana have a name?

- Which came first, the chicken or the egg?

- Does God think?

Your ability to ask, listen, look, and accept ambiguity works to stretch your brain muscles. Life can get pretty boring if all you have in your head is what you learned in school. If you drive the same route to work, watch the same TV programs, keep telling the same old jokes, how can you expect not to be bored or boring? Can't think of a gift to buy for your partner? Can't pick a restaurant? You're in a rut, pal. Time to clean out the warehouse.

And while you're at it, check out your most deeply held beliefs. I recommend always questioning about 20 percent of your beliefs. One of them should be a deeply held sacred cow. As you're questioning any belief, look for ways to deepen and enrich it. But don't be afraid to replace what needs replacing. Don't worry. If the belief is solid, based on solid ground, it will survive the scrutiny and stay in the warehouse. If not, you're better off without it.

FRESH VS. STALE

Great minds always stay nimble because they've learned how to move on. Einstein worked on big problems until he died. The artists we most admire transform themselves and their work from time to time. Here's a comparison of artists I find perpetually fresh. For every fresh artist I've named, I'll bet you can think of an artist that keeps dishing out warmed-over versions of the same old leftovers.

FRESH

☞ Bob Dylan drove his folkie fans to distraction when he came on stage with a rock band behind him. Since then he's broken new ground with every album.

☞ Madonna never bores, always surprise with zeitgeist.

☞ George Harrison continuously reinvented himself and his music, introducing us literally to new worlds of musical expression.

☞ Louis Armstrong taught the world to sing, invented scat, and blew the trumpet like no other since.

☞ Betty Friedan wrote the revolutionary book *The Feminine Mystique* in the '60s and ground-breaker *The Fountain of Aging* in the '90s.

☞ Andy Kaufman pushed the boundaries of comedy.

☞ U2 stays very cool and at the top of the charts after 22 years. Also involved with Amnesty International. Bono founded DATA (Debt, Aid, Trade for Africa).

☞ Stephen Soderbergh keeps films new.

☞ Howard Stern, now in his mid 40s, still keeps shocking us.

☞ VW brought back a cool, new Bug.

☞ Stephen King writes novels and short stories in different genres.

☞ George Carlin constantly develops new material.

☞ Andy Warhol changed forever the definition of "what is art?"

☞ Giorgio Armani kept fashion fresh for more than four decades.

☞ Sting was hot with The Police and now he's whit hot as a solo ballad-singer-composer.

- ☞ Lauren Hutton evolved from Playboy bunny to empowering menopausal women.

- ☞ Will Smith started as a rapper and developed into a serious actor.

- ☞ Hugh Hefner still gets the babes and throws parties that Gen X celebrities compete to attend.

- ☞ Carrie Fisher won acclaim as an actress, and then went on to be a bestselling author.

- ☞ Jerry Seinfeld canceled his own show while it was still popular.

- ☞ Billy Blanks turned what could have been a black version of Jack Lalane into an empire with a world training center, Billwear merchandise, the Billy Blanks Foundation, and Billy Blanks Enterprises.

BLOCK: Keep Your Nose to the Grindstone
BLOCKBUSTER: Space Out

What would your boss do if she caught you staring at the ceiling? If you're like Homer Simpson, responsible for monitoring a nuclear power plant, maybe you shouldn't be daydreaming. But if your job involves any kind of thinking, if you're responsible for coming up with new ideas, if it's your job to improve anything, you should spend some time each day spacing out.

> All things can somehow be linked together either in a physical, psychological, or symbolic way.
>
> — BUCKMINSTER FULLER

I'm not talking about wasting time. Just the opposite. Spacing out means taking total advantage of your brain's ability to make incredibly powerful fresh thoughts from random and diverse connections. But it can make these kinds of connections only when you let it have its way. Opening up your brain's total connection-making potential is what I call spacing out.

Earlier in this chapter I explained that your brain doesn't exactly work like a warehouse. What an understatement! Your brain is such a versatile organ. Rather than taking a picture of every scene in your life and storing it whole, your brain captures your sensations in parts. A fact, a face, a phone number, or a childhood memory, consists of a pattern of connections. And they're all interconnected. An odor can bring back to mind a song and the person you were dancing with.

When you remember, you don't pull a picture or a tape out of a file. It's more like reassembling the pieces. Sometimes during reassembly, related or unrelated parts get attached to the memory, like the way something smelled or the vividness of someone's dress the day of the memory. These additional parts might add to or detract from the initial purity of the memory.

This view of the brain provides clues to a number of riddles. Why each of us remembers a particular event so differently. Why a sensation might call up what seems to you an unrelated memory. Why your most brilliant ideas hit you in the shower or behind the wheel. How *déjà vu,* premonitions, and intuition might work. For our purposes, it clearly says pay attention to the pieces.

It might help to think of your brain as a sky full of stars and each star a piece of information. When you concentrate on something, it's like focusing on one star. When you think logically, you construct a constellation like Orion or the Big Dipper. When you space out, you create new constellations from stars anywhere in the entire sky. Of course, your brain has many, many more neurons to connect than visible stars in the sky.

With that in mind, it's easy to see how you can make new ideas out of any combination of ideas, but only when your brain recognizes them. In order to recognize ideas, you've got to space out and train your brain to accept what seems to be nonsense and turn it into sense. Making sense is the easy part. Accepting the idea that you can find sense in nonsense is the hard part.

You're alive today because, normally, your brain rejects nonsense. When you're driving down the street and get a sudden urge to play tennis, your brain says, "I'm going to backhand you if you don't keep hands on the wheel." Thank you, brain! This kind of thinking serves you well except when you're trying to break new ground.

EXERCISE
Shut Your Rut

To think out of a rut, you have to turn off the part of your brain that demands sense. Space out. Allow unusual thoughts, contradictions, and fuzzy thinking to play with each other. Take advantage of all the connections in all the space in your brain. What if you programmed some spacing out time in your day or in your employees' day? Would you and they come up with better ideas? You can count on it. Companies who take new product development seriously give their researchers time to work on projects that may or may not pay off. Give your speculative thinking some real respect. Why not mark some space out time on your calendar? You'll be surprised at what undirected, purely exploratory thinking does for your life.

EXERCISE
Eine's Boo-Boo

All knowledge is pliable. Like gold, the malleable precious metal, ideas can be shaped and adapted without losing and even increasing their value. The more ideas and information you hold in your brain, the more opportunities you have to make outstanding connections. Couple a sky full of brilliant ideas and stellar information with a spark plugged, pliable, nimble brain like Einstein's, and you get ideas that change the world.

Nevertheless, even Einstein fell into the trap of tossing out ideas that didn't seem to make sense. In 1917 he postulated that empty space is not totally empty, instead it has its own "invisible energy." This dark energy, he continued, would act like gravity in reverse, causing galaxies to repel one another rather than attract. Nah! Einstein dumped the idea, thinking it was just too weird.

New astronomical evidence, however, suggests not only that repulsion exists but also that it began to overwhelm gravity in the last few billion years, just as Einstein's theory stated. What else did Einie toss? What ideas have you tossed because they were simply too weird? What meetings have you attended where you bit your tongue at the risk of introducing an idiotic input? Weird? Idiotic? To whom? How many great ideas have died just because someone was afraid to offend the beliefs of a group?

PLIABLE KNOWLEDGE

Any piece of information is just that, a piece of information. It can be assembled with other pieces of information. Often these pieces fit well together, most of the time they don't. In either case, we never throw away the pieces. No! Keep them, because any piece of information can help build a new idea when it meets the right piece.

> There is much pleasure to be gained from useless knowledge.
>
> — BERTRAND RUSSELL

Let ideas live, serve them up, nurture them. It's never necessary to kill them— ever. And it can be so gratifying to pay them off. Let your ideas live so you can revisit them. Say them out loud, so other people can use them. Who gives a crap what others may be thinking! The idea of pliable knowledge says that your scrap heap of ideas forms a foundation that you or someone else can continuously build upon.

Learn to see more information than what appears on the surface. When you look at a picture, see the pixels not just the picture. Break everything into its elements. Reduce the entire world to its elemental parts—photons of light, notes of odor, frequencies of sound, vibrations of touch. Ask why. Why did Leonardo paint the *Mona Lisa*? What do you think her eyes say? Her hands—why do they rest that way? What music would go with viewing such a work of art? You may not find an immediate use for your speculations, but someday your thoughts may trigger a thought that absolutely amazes you.

The world is an infinite accumulation of information. You can connect any piece of information with any other piece of information at any time. Often these random combinations form original ideas. Many times they don't. But we never throw away the pieces. No! We keep them, because we know that any piece of information can help build a new idea. All knowledge can function as a base for new knowledge.

40 WINKS

Go to your boss today and ask her if she can help you become a much more effective thinker. She'd say, "Please, tell me how!" Your answer "Let me take a nap every day."

Napping has proved itself a powerful brain supercharger. When did we begin to equate naps with laziness? How many times have we bragged about how little sleep we received and still were able to perform? Well, it goes against the nature and the results from a 25-year study on the effects of napping. The study revealed that 92.5 percent of workers, after an afternoon nap,

> It takes a lot of time to be a genius. You have to sit around so much doing nothing, really doing nothing.
>
> — GERTRUDE STEIN

increased their productivity, their creativity, and their problem solving skills. Everybody say, "Siesta!"

Some of us got the idea. Dan Janssen, the speed skater, napped throughout his Olympic training. Brahms napped at the piano while composing a song that put us all to sleep at least once. Winston Churchill required a daily afternoon nap in order to cope with his wartime responsibilities, not to mention his frequent hangovers. Paul McCartney wrote two of his biggest hits right after a nap. Now they call him Sir.

So if you're a manager of a team and you want to make them more effective, send them to the break room and tell them to chill, meditate, do yoga, and take a nap. We're not talking about sawing logs, just take some time to lie down, stay quiet, and rest. The first higher-level manager who tries this in a Fortune 500 company will be on the cover of *Fast Company* for being an innovating expert or the *National Enquirer* charged with sexual harassment.

BLOCK: It's All About Me
BLOCKBUSTER: A Day in the Life

It's the mid-1960s. A young couple enjoys dinner and pleasant chitchat. If the woman seems distracted, it's because she's listening to both her husband and the washing machine downstairs. Suddenly a noise from the basement prompts her to run down the stairs and add fabric softener to the rinse cycle—a very crucial moment in those days. If you wanted your clothes to be soft and fragrant, you had to add liquid fabric softener at the right time.

Puzzled, the woman's husband, a Procter & Gamble chemical engineer, begins to ask himself a series of questions:

- Why must introducing the softener have such a small opportunity window?

- Why can't it be added before the wash in the pile of dirty clothes?

- Or could you add it after washing?

- What if you changed the form of the softener?

- Could the active ingredient release over time instead of at once?

- Why not soften clothes in the dryer?

- What if we name it "Bounce?"

CHALLENGE	SEE	SAW	RESULT
Stop washing interruptions	How to engineer solutions	A Day in the Life	Bounce

Okay, it didn't happen quite that fast, but this true story accurately illustrates how to find opportunities for improving the lives of those around you. When you feel someone's pain, you get beyond empathy to where opportunity lies. And let's face it, not every problem you face concerns only you. More often than not our problems get all tangled up with those around us—family, friends, coworkers. Working out these problems demands empathy. That's the ability to feel what someone else feels.

You can build empathy by imagining yourself going through someone else's life. As the saying goes, "by walking a mile in their shoes." At Marco Polo Explorers, we like to go even further and spend "a day in the life" of someone whose problems we're attempting to solve. When you live the life of a consumer and observe the hows and whys around what they do, fresh solutions abound.

As a child you found more wonder, you asked more questions, and caught more of the details you take for granted as an adult. Taking things for granted comes from seeing so many things so much more frequently. There's only one way out of this rut—deliberate attention, almost to the point of annoyance. Children in their pure inquisitiveness will find out what someone does and why. They'll ask, "Why did you do it that way?" As a child, you wonder why anyone has to be in any kind of pain or discomfort.

Notice how empathy ties back to the Support First technique from the previous chapter. It's easier to support someone if you feel how good that support feels. Or if you imagine how you would appreciate similar support.

Just as living a day in the life can uncover incredible marketing opportunities, it can help you understand and get along better with a troublesome coworker, demanding friend, or an obnoxious in-law. Typically, though, each of us lives in a personal vacuum, quick to offer solutions without knowing all the facts. It's no surprise, then, that instead of offering worthwhile solutions, we offer thin, ill-informed ones, if we offer anything at all.

EXERCISE
Making Empathy Pay

Empathy means really trying to understand what someone else goes through instead of how his or her behavior affects you. Sometimes this entails examining minute details of that person's daily activities. Just as the inventor of Bounce went through every mundane activity involved in softening a load of laundry. Spending time in the life of the people you live and work with will give you balance and help keep some perspective on life. Like a child who wants to comfort mommy when mommy's not feeling so good—the ability to feel someone else's pain will help you create positive impact.

Whose life should you spend time in? Your spouse, your kids, a close friend or lover? Follow their schedule. What do they absolutely have to get done today? Can you help? Your help might free them up to spend more time with you. What about at work? Your boss, a coworker, or someone who works for you? Think of how you can get into their shoes. Feel their pain and discomfort. Offer to help. Better yet, do something you know will help. The results will astound you.

BLOCK: Don't Mess With Success
BLOCKBUSTER: If It Ain't Broke, Break It

Can I get you to assume one thing? Life is change. Everything changes. What we believe today may not be true tomorrow. Nod and read on if you're in agreement. (If you don't agree, close this book now! It's too dangerous for you to read.)

If everything changes, what about the truths you hold most dear? Certainly some of them are absolute, immutable. But what if they're not? Could you handle it? What would throw you? How would you deal with it?

> Every act of creation is first of all an act of destruction.
>
> — PABLO PICASSO

Consider just a few of the long held truths we've been asked to discard during the twentieth century:

- A heavier than air machine cannot fly.

- Women can't be effective executives.

- Humans use only ten percent of their brains.

- You'll never see a black quarterback in the NFL.

- Intelligence is genetically determined.

- The United States has never lost a war.

- If you can't get pregnant, you have to adopt.

- You're old at 60.

- Women are the gentler sex.

- White men can't jump.

- Cars can only run on air polluting gas.

- When your vital organs go, your days are numbered.

- Disabled individuals are stuck living compromised lifestyles.

- People won't buy water in little bottles.

- Cloning human beings is impossible.

- We can't go to the moon.

- You have to have sex to have a baby.

- You can't have a phone in your car.

- You can't wear white after Labor Day.

- You have to stop your car to pay a toll.

- People will never pay more than a quarter for a cup of coffee.

- Women can't serve in active combat.

- Cancer is a death sentence.

- The Soviet Union is the United States' greatest enemy.

- We'll never live in outer space.

- Women over 45 can't deliver healthy babies.

- You can't fight City Hall.

- Europe will never unite under one currency.

- No late-night TV host will ever be as popular as Parr or Carson.

- There will never be a black Miss America.

- Everything that needs to be invented has been invented.

- Running a sub-four-minute mile is physically impossible.

If it hasn't already happened it will. One of these days something you hold to be a self-evident, absolute truth will turn out to be wrong. Surely you don't want to end up like those who had to be dragged kicking and screaming to the fact that the earth is not flat. So why not get ready? At least test your assumptions. Maybe you'll overturn something in the process of questioning your beliefs. Or if somebody else cracks one of your sacred cows, at least it won't come as a total surprise.

Engineers regularly do something called destructive testing. They determine the strength of materials by breaking them, based on the assumption that you can find out how strong something is only after you take it to the point of its own destruction. What better way to equip yourself for the ever changing world? Let's try it.

EXERCISE
Constructive Destruction

Take something you think is totally true and utterly destroy it. Tear it apart, examine it closely, break it in different ways, find out and record its limits. It's easy to destroy something you don't value. Start with a gold standard—Mt. Rushmore, motherhood, Elvis, organized religion, real men don't cry. The truth, the whole truth, and nothing but the truth, so help you.

Break your test subject into its elemental parts. Once you've got it in pieces, ask yourself how you might improve it, overcome its limitations. What would you do first? What parts belong? What can go? Which need to change? Put the pieces back together in new ways. Give it a facelift. Find new opportunities for different parts and combinations.

Go at it the way you did as a child, before you developed the restraint that comes from years of reinforcing a belief. Most of what kids destroy, they're seeing for the first time. So they're more likely to have a pliable understanding of what they see. That makes them more likely to bust it up. Pretend you're looking at your subject for the first time. Leave all of your assumptions behind.

Lorne Michaels, creator and executive producer of Saturday Night Live, rebuilt the program after purging its line up of stars, writers, and staff from the bottom up more than once. He came up with a better show almost every time. Okay, some will debate which crews were better than their predecessors, but SNL remains the longest running comedy show in the history of television. Not just the longest running live show.

Instead of waiting for a competitor to put us out of business, we at Marco Polo Explorers constantly challenge the effectiveness of our processes, beliefs, and methods. We break ourselves, in theory, to create a stronger set of ideals in the long run.

You can find the same kind of constructive destruction anywhere. I'm thinking cars that have undergone total overhauls—Bonneville, Corvette, Thunderbird.

Once you're good at this blockbuster exercise, you'll find you do it almost instantly when you have doubts about more mundane issues such as accepted business practices, relationship rules, and all kinds of conventional wisdom. The better you get at busting things up, the more quickly and easily you'll be able to turn uncomfortable or unacceptable situations into situations you can and want to handle.

EXERCISE
It Wasn't Me!

Somewhere along the way to adulthood we picked up the crazy idea that honesty is the best policy. I'm not so sure. Honesty lifts ordinary relationships to dizzying levels of love, but it can also kill romance. It could be downright cruel to answer, "Do you think I'm gaining weight?" with total candor.

It's just plain stupid to tell the whole truth when you're making a deal. Say you're shopping for a car and the salesperson asks you, "What are you really capable of paying?" Or suppose you've convinced someone to hire you and after you state your salary requirement, you're asked, "But how much money do you really think you can get by with?"

Ever hear of the show Kids Say the Darndest Things? It featured 4- to 8-year-old kids who displayed pure, unabashed honesty and the ultimate in bare-knuckled, lying-through-their-teeth storytelling. But from the kids' point of view, they weren't lying. They were giving the conversation the momentum of a flowing stream. They still had the makings of improvisational genius.

> Any fool can tell
> the truth,
> but it requires a man
> of some sense
> to know how
> to tell a lie well.
>
> — SAMUEL BUTLER

Lying is a great way to exercise your imagination. Comedian Jon Lovitz made a career out of lying with his Tommy Flanagan character, the pathological liar famous for, "Yeah, Yeah, that's the ticket!" This kind of harmless lying—so obvious that no one would ever believe you—forces you to invent facts rather than rely on what you know to be true. Lying, also known as exaggeration or embellishment, keeps the momentum of a good story even better. It prompts your listeners to challenge you either out of curiosity or suspicion. Lying forces you to shift your train of thought quickly, and inadvertently you may find a new way to attack a problem. It can also break down cemented beliefs. Why not tell a tall tale to explore the outer fringes of possibility? It's a great way to exercise your creative mind. It will sharpen your wits and better prepare you for the day you have to lie to save your skin. Start by stating the opposite of what you want to say. Then go with it. Let your imagination run as long as you think you can improvise before you start reeling your story back in toward the truth.

EXERCISE
Because I Said So!

You were having such a good time! Deeply entranced in something fun and frivolous. Suddenly your bubble burst when you heard, "Stop it!" And if you challenged your parents and asked why, they replied, "Because I said so!"

Tell a child no and you've got their attention, but that's all you've got. They'll look at you funny and say they heard you, but they have no intention of complying. Some adults feel that a spirited child must be beaten down with "No!" and "No!" again. Just like what they get in the rough adult world.

Adults have an acute understanding of what you can or cannot do, what the rules are, appropriate dress, conduct, and behavior. That's good. There are times when you have to protest, "Hey, that's not allowed!" A child doesn't like rules and often questions them. That's good, too. When an adult says no, it's to prevent trouble. When a kid says no, it opens new doors.

When you lived in the People's Republic of Mom and Dad, you followed their rules whether the rules made sense or not. Now that you're an adult, free to make your own rules, free to choose which rules you will or will not obey, you need to decide when to play it safe and when to challenge authority—your own authority or the authorities. The key is common sense. Picking your battles. Putting your foot down when the result promises to yield positive results.

But don't hesitate to say no just for the heck of it now and then. Rules and regulations actually condition us to be lazy. They discourage us from considering other options. So the next time someone tries to beat you down with a rule, a look, or a word of caution, tell them no. You're in for some mind-opening responses and results.

You may want to decide in advance what kinds of rules you're no longer going to follow. Dress code, punctuality, table manners? What do you expect to gain from rejecting such conventions? Keep in mind, there's a thin line between stupidity and constructive rebellion.

RAY CHARLES MUST BE GOD

> Animals, which move,
> have limbs and muscles;
> the earth has no limbs
> and muscles, hence
> it does not move.
>
> —SCIPIO CHIARAMONTI,
> Professor of Philosophy
> and Mathematics,
> University of Pisa, 1633

God is love.
Love is blind.
Ray Charles is blind
Therefore, Ray Charles must be God.

If this syllogism makes sense to you, congratulations! You're thinking like a four-year-old again. If it's merely funny—you just can't get your mind around a black, blues-singing god—we've still got some work to do. If it's not funny, we've got a lot of work to do.

Any logician will tell you that a syllogism is only as good as its premises. Start off with a false premise and you'll sink deeper and deeper into nonsense. But we value nonsense, right? All great, new-to-the-world ideas sound ridiculous until we get used to them. Like indoor plumbing. Great idea. But before it won wide acceptance as a necessity, how would you describe it to someone who never heard of it? Basically we're talking about bringing the outhouse into the house. What possessed someone to suggest such an idea? The chilly midnight sprint to the outhouse might suggest moving it closer, but the flies and the stink always argue for moving it away. Stalemate. Only kidlike naked thinking can get you out of it.

You can use your appreciation of nonsense to measure your naked thinking ability. If you can put unrelated facts together and come up with a new conclusion like Ray Charles is God, keep up the good work. If you find yourself doing it naturally, even better. You're starting to think like some of the world's greatest innovators. Keep dreaming up ridiculous ideas. One just may turn out to be the world's next necessity. Mess with logic. Take several statements assumed to be true and then make them collide to create a surprising and original conclusion.

We can become rigid in the way we look at the world and process information. This always leads to the same progression of thought. Summon your childhood sense of play and exercise your ability to make nonsense out of everyday facts.

The capital of South Dakota is Pierre
Pierre is a French pastry
French pastries taste good
Therefore . . .

EXERCISE
The "No" Hall of Fame

How many truly great people in history gained strength from the word no. Who fought the law because they saw a better way, a more equitable solution for everyone involved? Here follows my incomplete list of my most admired no-sayers.

- Sam Wyche and his Bengals said no mandatory huddles.

- Rosa Parks said no to riding in the back of the bus.

- Cesar Chavez said no to inhuman working conditions for migrant workers.

- Susan B. Anthony said no to political exclusion.

- Abraham Lincoln said no to slavery and splitting the union.

- Henry Heimlich said no to the Red Cross resuscitation procedure.

- Martin Luther King said no to racial segregation.

- Tommie Smith said no to the racial inequity in the United States

- Mahatma Gandhi said no to British domination of India.

- Christopher Columbus said no to falling off the edge of the earth.

- Munch, Picasso, and Pollack said no to the art trends of their day.

- Richard Simmons said no to the macho ideal of fitness.

- Einstein discarded the notion that time is a constant.

- Nelson Mandela said no to an all-white-ruled South Africa.

- Desmond Tutu said no to retribution.

- George Carlin said no to early broadcast censors.

- Lance Armstrong said no to being debilitated by cancer.

- Babe Ruth said no to "early to bed, early to rise" as the key to success.

- Frank Zappa said no to Tipper Gore and music industry censorship.

- Decca Records said no to signing The Beatles (whoops!)

Who's on your list? Who said no in an effort to improve the world some way? Describe what they did and how they overcame unacceptable rules. When do you find yourself saying yes when you should say no? Make a list. I'll get you started.

- Ice cream at midnight

- Buying on credit

- When your boss gives you more than you can do

- Watching TV instead of exercising

- Wasting time instead of reading

BLOCK: Everything's Copasetic
BLOCKBUSTER: Brain Wedgies

A Brain Wedgie does to your brain what a wedgie does to your butt. I borrowed the term *wedgie* from a prank designed to bring attention to the bottom of your anatomy. You get a wedgie when someone sneaks up behind you, grabs the waistband of your underwear, and yanks it up toward your head. The idea is to shake you up, get your attention, and move you to action.

Brain Wedgies throw you off-balance—out of that comfort groove your brain and butt have taken to. They stop you in your tracks and force you to look at what you've been doing and the way you've been thinking. They're nature's way of saying, "Hey, big shot, get a load of this!"

Let's face it, we'd all just plod along in life if it weren't for startling events like the loss of your job, a declaration of war, your best friend returning from Denmark with a "nip and tuck." Intelligent people recognize a Brain Wedgie as the jolt they need to redirect their attention and themselves. So why not perform Brain Wedgies on each other and ourselves for that purpose?

An event doesn't have to make you wonder if you should have gotten out of bed that morning to qualify as a Brain Wedgie. It could be a seemingly positive event, like getting promoted to a job with enormously expanded responsibilities. The kind of responsibilities that send you to the restroom and find you staring at yourself in the mirror wondering what the heck you've gotten yourself into.

It's nice to coast, to sail aimlessly on a rudderless ship, never really mapping out where we're headed. Nothing wrong with that. It just never lasts. Life-shaking events sometimes come with a warning, sometimes without, but they always come. They give some of us the jolt we need to direct ourselves. They give others hives, headaches, ulcers, or worse.

A Brain Wedgie deals in some way with things that you're not prepared to deal with. But they aren't always tragic. They do get your attention, stretch your mind, and force you to think differently. Here are two of my favorites:

1. How do people go to the bathroom? Our Marco Polo Explorers explored this subject on a project for Cottonelle. (By the way, are you a scruncher or a folder?)

2. I wore a sanitary napkin for five days, immersing myself in the use of the product and trying to find opportunities for new product development. Wearing a sanitary napkin is not a Brain Wedgie for a woman used to wearing the damn things, but to a man, it was both a physical and psychological wedgie. This Brain Wedgie was designed to open my eyes to new product development possibilities. Ideas that were pretty self-evident to me, a man, but not quite as evident to someone who has learned to live with the currently available options.

EXERCISE
Give Yourself a Wedgie

What would constitute a Brain Wedgie in your world? What would make you think differently? How would you adjust your life accordingly? It's easy to say you sympathize or feel someone's pain, but it's nothing like giving yourself the Brain Wedgie version. If you really want to know what your spouse goes through, walk in his or her shoes for a day. Want to feel what your kids feel? Attend their daycare center or school all day. Want to understand what homelessness is all about? Do it for a week.

Force yourself to experience the pain. You'll be in control of the situation, so you can limit the pain in time and intensity, but you'll still get a much better sense of someone else's point of view. Give yourself a Brain Wedgie to prepare yourself for trouble you might someday face—divorce, bankruptcy, or anything else you dread. Writing a living will or signing an organ-donor card forces you to face the ultimate Brain Wedgie.

When you have to face any of these dreaded events, you'll preempt some of the shock and find yourself better equipped to deal with things.

EXERCISE
Don't Put that in Your Mouth!

While you're out there testing life all over again with kidlike wonder, try startling your senses the way you did when you were too naïve to know better. Scientists know better. They analyze bird crap with chemicals and instruments. A kid will touch it, smell it, and even taste it. Who comes away with more useful information? The scientist, of course. But who gets to tell the best gross-out story? Who's more likely to come up with a recipe for Christmas cream drop cookies?

Do I want you to taste bird doo? No way. But I do suggest that you investigate the world with more than one or two of your senses. Don't assume you can't listen to a flower or that a rock doesn't smell like anything. Or that you can't eat dessert first, bark at a cat, lick the terminals of a 9-volt battery, study the rainbows in a CD, listen to a candle burn, feel the screen door, or smell this book.

When you're stuck on a problem of any kind, think of how you can investigate the situation with all your senses. What ideas does your multisensory investigation suggest? You'll be amazed at the power of understanding that every piece of stimulus can deliver. Suddenly lots of possibilities arise.

NO PAIN, NO GAIN

All of your learning as a kid came from direct experience. You had no language tapes or walking manuals. It was pure trial and error. You learned about hot by touching a stove. Maybe you smacked the dog and got nipped. Everything went into your mouth and sometimes, right back out. Yech!

You've heard all the clichés—what doesn't kill me makes me stronger, live and learn, behind every dark cloud there's a silver lining. The essential truth lies in each one of them. Life's best lessons come with some pain, but you have a chance to grow from every one of them. Because nothing teaches like pain.

My tae-kwon-do teacher warned me over and over again, "Keep your hands up!" I'd start each sparring session with hands high, protecting my face. Eventually they'd descend out of fatigue and cockiness. Maybe I thought I was Muhammad Ali. Then one night, sparring with a black belt, I got bopped on the nose. From then on my hands were high.

I'm not asking you to get punched in the nose or play chicken with death. Life will serve up its share of trouble. You don't have to go looking for it. But when you take your lumps, look for the lesson. Marie Curie lost her life introducing us to radioactivity. Magellan didn't get to complete his historic round trip. Surely you can get in there and get your hair messed up.

LOOK AT YOUR NEIGHBOR'S PAPER

```
                                    ☐ URGENT
To _____          A.M.
Date _____ Time _____           P.M.
      WHILE YOU WERE OUT
From _____ YOU FORGOT _____
Message _____

           If I have seen further
           it is by standing
           on the shoulders
           of giants.

           — ISAAC NEWTON
Signed _____
                              001 Reorder No.
```

Now that you understand how not to think, you're ready to begin thinking naked. This chapter will teach you how to cheat, a fundamental naked thinking habit. We'll start with why it's okay to cheat and then learn how to do it. Learning these techniques will give you the head start you need to make cheating as natural as breathing.

- **LIFE IS AN OPEN BOOK TEST** explains why it's smart, fun, and good to cheat.

- **WHY, WHY, WHY** gives you the key to simplifying your problems with one word.

- **HIS TRUCK IS BETTER** helps you decide which neighbor's paper to look at.

- **DOUBLE IT OR ADD A ZERO** shows you how to surround yourself with options by attacking problems with abundance.

- **DNA** explains why you should use people and the unique things they bring to your party.

- **DRESS UP** presents the benefits of immersing yourself in the problems you want to solve.

- **LET THE FORCE BE WITH YOU** is all about going with the momentum of the world around you.

- **TRIP TO THE ZOO** shows you how to find strategic brilliance in nature.

- **SQUARE PEG, ROUND HOLE** encourages you to use unconventional, even radical sources of inspiration.

- **UBERKID** offers a final word on the necessity and value of practice.

Remember, at the beginning of the book, we discussed the boneheaded idea of toughing it out? Well, let me tell you that toughing it out becomes triple hard to take when it affects others.

Let's suppose I decided to tough it out in order to write this book. It might improve my writing skills, and I might get better at organizing my thoughts, but at what expense? I'd have a hard time finding a publisher. If I published it myself, it might prove painful for you to read. So it would make a ton of sense for me to get some help, right?

When I thought about writing this book, I made a checklist of what I felt would make it an important book. I did a ton of research and paid colleagues to do the same. I measured the effectiveness of my Think Naked principles on my family, friends, and even some foes (unbeknownst to them). I watched children at play and read about their behavioral traits and innate intelligence. Then I locked myself in a room in front of a computer and started to write. Blah, blah, blah... Yech! I found out that I could think naked out loud, but it didn't translate to the page.

In short, I understood that I needed to *cheat*! Yes, I needed to look at my neighbor's paper in order to adequately convey what thinking naked could mean to people. So I faced my fear of ridicule and self-pride and decided to find some collaboration.

Remember the Monster Under the Bed technique? Instead of going through the pain of trying to write this book on my own, I faced my fear, acknowledged it, recognized my limitations, and attacked the writing monster. As it turned out, the monster wasn't an abhorrent, knife-wielding thug. It was merely the fear of denying what I knew to be true.

If I had denied what made me afraid, the denial would have ultimately ruled me. I would have remained one of those people who spends his life talking about the book he's writing. Instead, I started talking to my colleagues. I needed someone who would be selfless in helping me write what I had in mind—a student of the mind and creativity. Someone who could organize all the information I had collected, express it clearly, and still preserve my voice. It didn't take long to find him. I enlisted the help of super creative, nationally renown naked thinker Peter Lloyd.

PETER: It's "renowned" not "renown."

MARCO: See what I mean? I need your help!!!

PETER: One exclamation point will do, by the way.

MARCO: Okay, smart guy! Don't make me regret this. I've been writing this book for two years. And as I read over my notes for this chapter called "Look at Your Neighbor's Paper," I realized I had to take my own advice.

PETER: You want to look at my paper?

MARCO: Figuratively, yes. But more than that.
I want to leverage your brilliance and will to cre-
ate. I know you're one of this country's foremost
authorities on creativity and innovation, and
I want to cheat off a really smart kid. You see,
I learned the value of cheating the hard way.
Remember when I was named one of America's
top Out-of-the-Box Thinkers?

PETER: You were a runner up, not numero uno.

MARCO: Right, during the final interview
process, one of the judges asked what made me
such an original thinker. I answered, "I cheat."

PETER: Judges hate cheaters.

MARCO: No kidding. Talk about getting "The
Look"! They obviously wanted a thinker whose
answers fit within their box. They had an ideal
version of what the winner would be like and it
wasn't me. It should be someone with all the
out-of-the-box answers in their head.

PETER: So who ended up winning the out-of-the-
box award?

MARCO: A woman who set up this running club
for underprivileged girls, a formidable task. She
had done great things for her community. When
she started crying during her interview, I knew
it was all over. I did get second place for expos-
ing myself in diapers I'd fashioned the night
before to demonstrate my Think Naked philosophy.
I got my picture taken with Dennis Rodman,
Marisa Tomei, and a slew of other celebs.
I scored spots on CNN, Showtime, and in the

National Enquirer. And they gave me a Mazda Protégé for a year.

PETER: I remember. You ended up with more press than the winner.

MARCO: Yeah, but my mother was mortified with the whole diapers in the *National Enquirer* thing. She expected so much more from her firstborn. Still, coming in second did nothing to discourage me from cheating. In fact, I've become even more convinced. Looking at my neighbor's paper remains one of my core values and the subject of this chapter. Cheating separates the quick from the dead. So, stick around, I'm sure I'll need you.

LIFE IS AN OPEN BOOK TEST

When did you realize some people are smarter than you? For some of us, it's pretty hard to admit. But it's true for all of us. It doesn't make you an idiot. Heck, with the exception of Einstein, da Vinci, Vos Savant, and a few others, we're all in the same boat. No matter how smart you are or think you are, there's always someone smarter. That goes for just about all your qualities—brains, brawn, and beauty. You name it. There will always be someone "er" than you.

> I have never let my schooling interfere with my education.
>
> — MARK TWAIN

So what are we going to do about it? Some of us admit our limitations and look for ways to overcome them, to even up the odds. The rest, smug and satisfied, keep falling behind without even realizing it. Their hardwired brains tell them they're doing just fine. You,

on the other hand, having read the blockbuster chapter, know you can break some rules. You're ready to give yourself an advantage over people who know more than you do. And you learned the secret in grade school—look at your neighbor's paper.

You weren't allowed to look at your neighbor's paper in school, although you may have tried. Your school was required to see if you could spit back what they had just attempted to drill into your head. If you looked at your neighbor's paper (a pretty resourceful way of giving them what they wanted), they had to flunk you. "I don't want to know what your neighbor knows, Mr. Marsan," Sister Mary Constipata used to tell me, "I want to know what *you* know."

In the rough, adult world, no one measures your ability to accumulate and regurgitate information anymore. Today the tests you take are for real. No more practice quizzes. It's all one big final exam. And you don't have to pull every answer, idea, or solution out of your head. Your boss, your spouse, your kids don't care where you get answers. They just want a solution that makes them happy. So even though it's difficult to believe this after more than a decade of education, here it is straight up: If you don't know the answer, it's okay to get it from somewhere else. It's smart to cheat.

IT'S SMART TO CHEAT

> Keep on the lookout for novel and interesting ideas that others have used successfully.
>
> – THOMAS EDISON

What makes someone smart? Is it their ability to memorize or to utilize? I think you know the answer. A recent study of brain activity shows that smarter people actually use less of their brains to solve a problem than slower people do. Makes perfect sense. It's not what you know, it's how you use what you know. For example, you can sit and add up a long column of numbers the way you were taught in second grade or you can group all the number pairs that equal ten, add them up, then add on the leftovers.

Smart people invent shortcuts. The brilliant physicist Richard Feynman contributed much to science in the way of shortcuts and simplification of very complex ideas. But he didn't stop there. He used clever math tricks to impress other scientists and help enhance his genius image. Feynman would set his watch behind by some odd number of hours and minutes—one hour and 37 minutes, let's say. When someone asked him the time, he'd look at his watch, pretend to be calculating, and reply, "An hour and 37 minutes ago it was . . ." Then he'd read out the time on his watch. Feynman wasn't just smart, he cheated really smart people into thinking he was smarter than he really was.

Celebrities cheat all the time. Do you really think your favorite talk show hosts know everything they spout off? No way. Researchers who supply them with all sorts of crib notes back them. Those seemingly all-knowing talking heads on the news, they're reading! Your doctor consults with other doctors. The President fills his cabinet with advisors. Heck, one time I even caught one of my Explorers practicing his Irish accent in order to better crack me up with one of his jokes!

You don't think I knew everything in this book, do you? Not a chance. It's full of stuff my staff and I dug up from all over the place. My publisher, editor, friends, and family all let me look at their papers.

Whenever I'm stuck for an idea, I cheat. I'll bring in a slew of people who think differently than I do—experts, textperts, choking smokers, consumers, artists, writers, fighters, old lamplighters—anyone who can give me a new, fresh perspective. Smart people look up, around, on their neighbor's paper—anywhere for suggestions, answers, and to stimulate their thinking. You knew that. So why would you hesitate to get the same kind of help?

There's no future in the Puritanical, macho game of knowing all the answers. It's more important to know how to get options than to know the answer. That's what they should have taught you in school. But it's not too late. Look in books, magazines, newspapers, and search the Internet. Ask your boss, spouse, coworkers, friends, or someone on the street. Use e-mail, phone, and pager, even snail mail. But learn how to cheat. Make it a reflex. The next time someone asks you something and you're not sure of the answer, tell him or her to wait while you look at your neighbor's paper and get back to him or her.

IT'S GOOD TO CHEAT

A lot of bad connotations come with the word *cheat*, you know? It connotes robbing the system, cutting corners, and doing things that Jimmy Stewart wouldn't consider. Why use it? Well, it got your attention, didn't it? I mean to shock a bit. But more to drive home the idea that you shouldn't settle for what you know or merely conventional sources of help. Step over the line and get more than the next person.

> Originality is nothing but judicious imitation.
>
> – VOLTAIRE

And that's not always really cheating, but it's the way breakthroughs get done. Every so-called original thought modifies one or combines two or more established thoughts. If you want to come up with new and original thinking, then start with what came before you. But don't stop there. Do more research, ask a ton of questions, test theories incessantly, make mistakes, and cheat as much as you can. Don't cheat on your taxes, but take all the advantages you can. Then try some that might be a little more imaginative. Don't cheat on your spouse. Don't cheat anybody. If anything, give more of yourself than you take. But don't hesitate to stretch the boundaries, bend the rules, or give yourself every honest advantage you can. Then bend some more.

I can see one of my readers in court now testifying, "Marco Marsan said it was okay to cheat on my taxes." So I'll repeat myself. Cheating on friends and family—bad. Cheating as in looking at your neighbor's paper, understanding the value of your predecessors, your competitors, recognized gold standards or case studies to understand that you don't have all of the answers—good. You have such opportunity when you leverage other thinking styles. If you want to validate a solution, ask people who think like you. If you want new answers and possibilities, ask people who don't think like you. Understand the value of diversity. Learn how to build on what came before you. Instead of disdain for a competitor, leverage what they can teach you. Use their momentum. Go outside of your category. Understand and use intelligence.

IT'S FUN TO CHEAT

I could have called this book *Applying the Advantages of Uninhibited Thinking to Your Life and Work*, but I wanted to drive home the idea that childlike thinking not only gives you great advantages, but it's fun, damn it! And I know that people who are having fun come up with more ways to live better. More ways to eliminate fear, embarrassment, even desperation.

> Good swiping is an art in itself.
>
> — JULES FEIFFER

If I had used the square title, maybe a few knuckleheads would have bought the book, read about cheating, and discarded it in anger and disgust. I named it *Think Naked* so people with a sense of humor and a streak of rebellion would pick it up and do something positive with their lives. So don't let me down now—get hung up on the idea of cheating. Playing by the rules dooms you to dullsville. Cheating gives you many more interesting options.

IT PAYS TO CHEAT

What if I told you that after a night at the blackjack tables you'd be $50,000 ahead? If I guaranteed it, would you listen?

Cheating is like a guarantee to win. Figure it out. If you take the best of what's already been discovered, what's already known, and improve it, how can you lose? Cheating isn't a deficiency, it's an efficiency. And what an amazing trick for those of us who aren't natural born rocket scientists— permission to cheat! We were taught to know the answer. Now we can keep crib notes.

> Honesty is the best policy— when there is money in it.
>
> — MARK TWAIN

Cheating doesn't mean getting lazy. It means getting to work. Doing better research, getting second and third opinions, always checking your thinking with smarter people and people with different points of view, and measuring your work against best practices. It takes time and sweat. It can be tedious, too, but it will help you create better solutions. How could it fail? Cheating puts a solid foundation under your efforts. You'll produce more options, solutions, and results if you first discover what you don't know and then fill in the blanks. This way, the road to an answer will always be different, affording you more tidbits of stimulus along the way. (Meanwhile you can do some Freshness Dating, the blockbuster I introduced in Chapter 5.)

When you cheat, there can never be a problem you can't optimize. Here are a few ways to help you make cheating a habit.

WHY, WHY, WHY,

Kids use one of the most effective cheating devises ever invented. Driven by the most innocent curiosity, they ask and ask and ask, "Why?" This simple technique gives you a tortoise and hare head start. If you use it wisely, you almost have to try to lose.

Studies indicate that children ask about 125 questions per day, while adults ask an average of six. Okay, some of their questions test us a bit, but there's brilliance in their innate impulse to ask, "What's that? Where are we going? Who did it?" At some point they start asking why. "Why" questions call for answers that reveal underlying causes, motivations, and reasons. When you repeatedly ask why, each *why* reduces your issue to a simpler state until it becomes elemental and much easier to solve.

When all diapers were shaped like rectangles, my dad, a Procter & Gamble inventor-researcher, asked why. He kept asking why. Why is the crotch as wide as the waist? Humans just aren't built like that. The result—the hourglass shape, a design that revolutionized the disposable diaper category.

This process also helps make sure you're working on the right problem. It often uncovers issues you can resolve along the way, leaving you with the problem that when solved will have the greatest effect. *Why* helps bust blocks. Asking why shows that you're wearing your cape and feeling safe enough to challenge what everyone else assumes to be true. Talk about superhero courage! It takes courage to admit you don't know the answer.

Asking why over and over challenges beliefs, assumptions, taboos, and blocks, opens new doors, uncovers hidden agendas, finds forks in the road, and reveals new avenues to pursue. Eventually you get to the lowest common "duh"-nominator— a revelation so obvious you wonder why the heck you didn't think of it before. It's like a damn miracle drug! Remember the inventor of Bounce, who asked why adding fabric softener had to fit into such a small time window. He kept asking why until he got to the now obvious solution. Duh!

Careful. We adults ask questions that are really statements. We make comments colored in our dyed-in-the-wool beliefs. We solve problems and look for solutions through our individual personal filters. Kids ask why because they really don't know. They ask real, naïve questions looking for straight, honest answers. When you ask why as sincerely and innocently as a child, you're setting yourself up for what may be some belief challenging discoveries.

WHY WAIT?

Edward Land developed the Polaroid instant camera when, after taking his daughter's picture, she asked, "Why can't we see the picture now?" Land and his family were on vacation in Santa Fe, New Mexico. He began to explain the process of photography to the little three-year-old, but he stopped and asked himself. "Why not?"

On a walk through the enchanted city, it's said the 34-year-old Land invented the Polaroid instant photography system in his head. Of course, it was easier for him than it would be for you or me. Land had already dropped out of Harvard and developed the first, modern light-polarizing filters for sunglasses, car headlights, and 3-D photography. He was primed.

But would Land have invented instant photography—first in sepia, then black and white, then color, followed by a long list of newer and cooler models—if his daughter hadn't asked why? Or if he had blown off her question as naïve and given her a fatherly lecture about patience? I don't think so.

HIS TRUCK IS BETTER

Before you look at anyone's paper it makes sense to do some comparison-shopping. Whose paper should you copy? In school, you want to cheat off the kid most likely to get an A. If you copy a kid who's just doing a little better than you, you won't do much better. When you copy, you don't always get all the answers copied right. And if the B-student has a bad day, you might not even get a C. So you copy off the very best and give yourself the best shot.

Now let's apply this to the rough, adult world. A lot of people try to solve their problems alone, in a personal vacuum. We know better, right? But even when some folks know they have to think differently or out of the box, they don't explore ideas outside their comfort zone. That would be like a boy not copying off the girl next to him because, "Yech! She's a girl." Face it, people who are different, even those we despise or whose beliefs we loathe, can still be a big help. You want to copy off the best, period, not just the best within your comfort zone.

COPY CATS

There just aren't a lot of totally original thoughts:

- The Beatles started out by singing cover tunes.

- Bach went blind in his old age copying scores of other musicians for personal study.

- Thomas Jefferson copied off of the Magna Carta when he wrote the Declaration of Independence.

- Roman leather bottoms from the beginning of the first millennium inspired the inventor of the bikini.

- The good ol' Pony Express of the wild west was first thought up in Persia around 500 B.C.E.

- Microsoft copied most of Windows from Apple.

- The United States is just Canada with guns and better music.

- Recycling copies what Mother Nature does on a daily basis.

- Junk bonds copy Wimpy—that plump character from Popeye cartoons said, "I'll gladly pay you Tuesday for a hamburger today!"

- The Coen brothers based their film, *O Brother, Where Art Thou?* on *The Odyssey.*

- *The Flintstones* were a stone-age version of *The Honeymooners.*

- *West Side Story* was *Romeo and Juliet* with singing and dancing.

- 'N Sync is a copy of Back Street Boys is a copy of New Kids on the Block is a copy of Menudo is a copy of The Monkees . . .

DOUBLE IT OR ADD A ZERO

Most of us have been taught to make do—waste not, want not. Kids know better. They can't get enough of any good thing. The world economy should get down on its knees and thank them. Without kids and other young at heart consumers clamoring for newer and better models, more colors, more sizes, and more forms of every conceivable version, set, and combination of hot new products, we could not live in such abundant prosperity. Without more, life would be like prison. Anyone who's ever lived in a controlled economy will back me up.

Anyone who's ever eaten at the Marsan home knows about more. I think most Italian households share the same reverence for abundance. I grew up in a home where, if the U.S. Army just happened to drop by during dinner, everyone would have plenty to eat, and then some. During Christmas, some of the homes on our street lit up like a cheesy Website. I swear, if someone had come by and stolen half their lights and decorations, no one would notice. When you surround yourself with plenty, you learn to appreciate the value of options. I want to show you how that applies to loading your life with positive choices.

> Anything worth doing is worth doing to excess.
>
> — EDWIN H. LAND

Psychologists tell us that when we face serious danger, like coming face to face with a tiger, we experience a reaction called "fight or flight." Not nearly enough choices. Neither option offers much comfort either. No wonder we panic. I'm telling you that you can fill your personal arsenal with many more choices. And when you do, it's like eating at Marsan's. "Pass the pasta . . . Somebody give that tiger a meatball . . . You need more wine?"

Think abundance. Surround yourself with options. You will attract more options if you are more than generous with your favors. When asked to bring a six-pack to the party, double it—bring two. Your friend asks you to help him move, add a zero—show up with a truck, duct tape, two handcarts, a bunch of boxes, and your buddy built like a gorilla. Don't get caught short. If you think you'll need ten dollars, bring a hundred.

In my first draft of this part of the chapter, I called this principle *Double It*. But then I took my own advice and doubled it. Now it's *Double It or Add a Zero*. I was thinking more and then some. Double your options or multiply them by ten. Don't stop there, though.

Take whatever you're doing and do more.

Don't think, "They're getting twice the work out of me, but they're paying me the same as somebody who's doing half the work." Understand that you're learning twice as much and getting twice as good. If you work for someone else, you're doubling your chances of a raise or a promotion. When it comes time to cut staff, who might be the last to go? If you work for clients, whom will they most likely call next time? Someone else or you who gave them twice what they expected? Over deliver! If two tickets to a James Brown concert are great, then hire a limo, wear a leopard skin cape and the night becomes historical. (Make that hysterical.) Ow! I feel good!

Don't think I'm asking you to be a totally self-sacrificing Mother Teresa. Just the opposite. By always giving more than expected, you're setting yourself up for always getting more. When you need help, you should have more help choices than you know what to do with. And even if you don't, remember, your range of options grows with experience. The more you do, the more you learn, the bigger your bag of experience. What a way to cheat!

When my divorce went through and the judge determined the amount of time I could spend with my son, I decided (thank you for your learned opinion) to do triple time—taking the time we were allotted and making it deeper, more meaningful and memorable. For us that meant hiking, biking, joking, poker, laughing, playing air guitar, Parcheesi, chess, checkers, backgammon, movies, singing, dancing... We made sure we didn't waste the time we spent together.

Any time you're handed a hard and fast rule that limits you, figure out a way to make the most of what you've been given. After all, there's already one thing you can have only one of and that's your life. So cram it with more choices. You'll make it much more livable.

CHILD SUPPORT

I was listening to a divorced dad complain about child support. He was all ticked off, because once a week he had to pay his ex-wife a sum of money. Real adult issue. How to think naked? Double it! Pay more less often. Eliminate some of half the writer's cramp by writing a check every two weeks. Better yet, every month. Heck, add some zeroes and pay once a year. Sure it'll still hurt, but only annually.

Next I gave him a Brain Wedgie: "Imagine your ex-wife gone forever. No more. The kids are now your responsibility. So start looking for decent daycare. Have you priced childcare lately? Then consider hiring the least expensive? What are the chances that the caregivers there will love your kids? I mean, the way your wife does. What would it be worth? What would you pay someone to love your kids as much as your wife does? Your former wife, God bless her, loves your kids. Price it out. Now compare that to the child support you're currently paying."

While he did the math, I waited. When I saw he got the message, I told him, "Go call your former wife and let her know how much you appreciate all the money she's saving you."

DNA

You've heard someone say, or maybe you've said, "I'm so busy, I wish I could clone myself." Maybe your boss complimented you, "We could use a few more just like you." I don't think so. Nothing personal, but that would be a mistake. You need more people *not* like you. That's not an insult. Read on.

Imagine yourself in your Happy Place. The scene is just the way you want it—maybe birds singing in the background, bright colors all around, or the smell of jasmine in the air. Whatever you prefer. Everything's perfect, except that you're alone. Now let's say I can deliver six clones of yourself or six of your best friends. Which do you choose? That was too easy.

The same goes for dealing with life's difficulties. If I asked you and your clones to create something new and useful, you'd all come up with the same ideas. But what if I gave you the proprietor of a bed and breakfast, a Tahitian coconut farmer, a Buddhist monk, a cellar-door salesman, Chrissie Hynde of the Pretenders, and a podiatrist? I think the seven of you might come up with some interesting stuff. Diversity makes the world a whole hell of a lot more interesting.

Each of us has our own distinct way of thinking. That is, a Distinct Neuron Archetype or DNA. (Not to be confused with Deoxyribose Nucleic Acid, your genetic blueprint contained in every cell of your body.) The DNA I'm talking about is your unique mind-set, the unique way neurons have assembled based on your upbringing, your personal experiences, dreams, and aspirations. Your DNA determines your unique way of processing information and stimuli.

I intentionally take the risk of confusing DNA (Distinct Neuron Archetype) with DNA (Deoxyribose Nucleic Acid). I want to emphasize what they have in common. Both are complex arrangements of many, many little bits of information. Both use that information to do incredible things. One builds your body, including your brain, and the other is what your brain becomes. From now on I'll be talking about Distinct Neuron Archetype, but please keep the similarities in mind.

Your Distinct Neuron Archetype represents the absolutely unique essence of who you are. It's your brain's architecture. It determines the way your brain works, what and how you think. And it's alive, always changing, forever making new connections. Even when you're sound asleep, your Distinct Neuron Archetype continues to fire off electrical impulses in your brain in a way that's different from anyone else on the planet.

Okay, that's the new kind of DNA, but why is it so important to thinking naked? Because you can share it. You might call sharing DNA a conversation, a phone call, or an e-mail. We're sharing DNA with this book. That is, you're getting some of my DNA. (Don't get any in your eyes!) Your DNA will be different from now on. When you talk with anyone, see a movie, listen to the radio, and read a billboard—your DNA changes. It's easy to see why your DNA is so unique. Why the next person's is so different. And what a powerful force can flow from combining them.

For example, you might think of a writer as someone who sits alone all day and hammers away at a keyboard. I did. Some writers do write alone but just as many hobnob, confab, and koffee klatsch their way through their work. It's hard—damn hard—to sit here and write about naked thinking for five or six hours a day. The very idea of spending hours working alone discouraged me from writing for some time. Then I realized I didn't have to write alone. I could cheat.

Back in the *Blockbuster* chapter I promised how powerful the brain chain reaction can be when you include other people. Now I'm telling you. When you limit your thinking to your own DNA you can get great results, but when you mix in the DNA of other brains, your results multiply exponentially.

EXERCISE
Your DNA Hit List

I cheat wherever possible. I actually have a list, a DNA Hit List, of people with their phone numbers and e-mail addresses. Each person on my list is the best I have found in their respective disciplines. There isn't a person on it that I wouldn't want in my mental sandbox when I start inventing.

Make a list of people you can use to amplify and enhance your own DNA. Include people from all walks of life. Make your list as diverse as possible. Include people who disagree with you, people whose interests reach far beyond yours. Limit it only to clever, honest folks, with pure intent. You might even get your most trusted friends to make the same kind of list, and then share lists.

I've started you off with a few categories. Obviously there are many more areas in your life where good DNA can help you. List them, too. Then enter the name, phone number, and e-mail address of the person you choose as your DNA in each category. Keep this list handy. When you need to look at someone's paper, go to your DNA Hit List and get help.

If you're not used to making lists, you might think this process feels contrived, but at least make the list. The first time you find your-self needing help, you might even tough it out instead of calling for help from your DNA List. Eventually, you'll begin to use your list and lose your habit of toughing it out. You'll start to develop a reflex, one that goes contrary to the "tough it out" reflex you've spent years being taught.

As you create your DNA hit list, call each of the people you iden-tify. Let them know you've added them as an invaluable resource. They will feel honored you asked them to be on your list.

CATEGORY	NAME	PHONE NUMBER	E-MAIL ADDRESS
Health			
Wealth			
Music			
Spiritual			
Auto Repair			

DRESS UP

Old folks don't have much interest in pretending to be someone else. Okay, maybe at Halloween or Mardi Gras. They know it's just a temporary disguise and the real world awaits them after the mask comes off. On the other hand, kids love to play roles. Tell them to act like a dog and, *Bam!* They drop to their hands and knees and start barking. Who's likely to get a better sense of dog-ness?

There will be times when the prize goes to the contender who most clearly understands some specific group of people. It happens all the time in marketing. But it can happen in any work, community, or family endeavor. It's always important to feel and understand the position of someone or some group you need to work with, live with, be married to, or do business with. It's all about empathy. *You can cheat your way to greater empathy by dressing up.*

The idea is to use stimulation that will help you understand someone else's motivation. What do they feel? How do they feel? How do they live, buy, work, and play? What do they believe and hold dear? What are their complaints and questions, loves and fears? The trick is to be that person. Walk in their shoes. Touch, taste, see, hear, and smell as much of their life as you can. Add accessories to make it real. Dress the part, then play the part. After you've played a part, record what you learned. Have someone question you. Dig for real insight into the other life. You'll be absolutely amazed with what you learn. You'll sharpen your intuition beyond what you can record, so be ready to trust your instincts. Don't just follow what you're able to record on paper.

LET THE FORCE BE WITH YOU

Forces come in all shapes and sizes. Some help you; others work against you if you let them. When I talk about "the force," I mean any or all of the forces affecting you at the moment. Someone else's attitude about you is a force that might inhibit you. Years of beliefs driven into your head can also inhibit you. On the other hand, someone's approval and your openness to new ideas is a force that can help you.

> You can plan
> a pretty picnic
> But you can't
> predict the weather
>
> — OUTKAST

But the force might also be a ball flying through the air, a punch coming toward your face, a recently popularized celebrity or event, a fad or a trend, a new drug or a clinical breakthrough, the weather, your health, and so on. Letting the force be with you means taking anything that's going on and using your insight, forethought, and timely reaction to make it work to your advantage.

The water the hydroelectric plant turns into electric energy that powers your lights, heat, air conditioner, dishwasher, and computer amounts to a force working in the background to help you. The engineers who designed the plant, made it possible for the enormous power in a river to turn the turbines that produce electricity. They also exploited the forces of magnetism; the way wire conducts electricity, the momentum of the turbine wheels, and on and on. Engineers understand natural forces and exploit them.

CHALLENGE	SEE	SAW	RESULT
Generate electricity	Waterfalls	Let the Force Be with You	Hydro-electric power

Your friends and other people who have a lot in common with you—your peers—make up a force that affects the way you behave. Depending on who they are and how they act, they can persuade you to behave honestly and with mutual respect or just the opposite. Peer pressure can be as positive as group therapy or as negative as mob rule. Ever wonder how whole societies can turn into genocidal maniacs? Demagogues understand social forces and exploit them.

Kids can't help but deal more naturally with the force. When they get tired, they drop. Unlike adults who belittle sleep and push themselves insanely forward, half-blind with impaired judgment. You're never going to beat any force of nature, but you can cheat a little. In judo, you use the momentum of your opponent. In life, you're way ahead of the game when you go with the immutable laws and forces of nature. You'll certainly beat those who try to fight them.

The idea is to understand the forces at work around you, determine which forces you want to use just the way they are and which you have to work with. Why go head to head with something that has a full head of steam? It's better to use the force to your advantage, to create something forceful with the energy that's coming at you. For example, remember The Memo from Chapter 2?

Dick's dismissal of me created a force that I could either fight or smile and use to my advantage. In addition to working around it and not fighting it, I later realized I could use it in my book as a story, an example of using someone's aggression to achieve a positive result.

I'm always reminded of the force when I see a wave start from the initiative of a few fans in a packed stadium. When a wave comes your way, you can either help it along or ignore it. It reminds me that we're all part of the force. When you aid the wave, you don't just add one pair of arms, you inevitably influence some people around you. Your part is important. Always. Just like Jimmy Stewart in *It's a Wonderful Life,* the force is also something that would not have happened if you hadn't gotten involved.

For some reason I'll never understand, I wanted to create the world's biggest chicken dance. Don't ask me why. I could have attempted to recruit thousands of dancers, supplied the music, rented the space, courted the press, and so on. Instead I followed forces already in place. I literally found a mob of people who had already downed a few brewskis and were already dancing to a Polka band at Cincinnati's annual Oktoberfest. All I had to do was wire the streets for sound and convince the revelers to do the chicken dance. How hard is that? Hiring a kid in a huge chicken suit didn't hurt either. For a while I held the world record for staging a 48,000 person chicken dance. Then someone came along, looked at my paper, found a similar force, and topped our world record. Neither of us would have held the world record without feeling and using the forces already in play.

STRATEGIC STIMULATION

The following techniques give you specific ways to cheat using existing forces. I've developed them based on my experience generating ideas for leading companies. The first force is strategic stimulation. I know that when people brain chain on their own, some do pretty well. When they brain chain in groups, they do a lot better. When they brain chain alone or in groups with strategic stimulation, they really score. It's all in the strategic stimulation.

Strategic stimulation is simply looking at the paper of the neighbor who's already been there or someplace similar. For example, when I'm helping a client create a new package for one of their products, I study the packaging of leading cosmetics, software, health and beauty aids, candy, breakfast cereal . . . wherever packaging innovation happens. But I also look in unexpected places: How do Jaguar dealers "package" their showrooms? How did Martin Luther present his 95 Theses? I might look at an origami Website, the Boy Scout Handbook knots section—anything to do with enclosing and presenting stuff.

You can do the same with any problem you're working on. If you want to be a better lover, for example, you can go to the typical sources—pick up any *Cosmopolitan* magazine, watch *Austin Powers*, read *Dating for Dummies*. Then reach further and study Shakespeare's sonnets and the *Kama Sutra*, read the love letters of King Henry VIII and Catherine of Aragon, or see the movie *Sex and Zen*. Think beyond human love and consider the mating rituals of the sexiest animals. Animals do some pretty outstanding things to impress and care for each other—grooming, singing, strutting, and sharing food. A lot of love and affection goes on between pet lovers and their pets. What can you borrow?

You see where we're going. And you can see how your options expand and how fresh and original they can be when you use strategic stimulation. If you want your options to take you beyond the expected, beyond incremental improvement, you've got to think like a kid and play outside your neighborhood.

TRIP TO THE ZOO

What do a 200-degree beetle fart, a burr, a cockroach, and an armadillo have in common? Give up? The letter *R*! Just kidding. They all possess some form of strategic brilliance. The bombardier beetle mixes two chemicals inside its rear end. And when they mix, they explode out in a boiling hot spray? It's one hell of a defensive weapon. It blinds its enemies with its spray.

Scientists at Case Western Reserve used this mixing strategy to improve a process where they used to mix ingredients and stir them in vats. Now they blend them in a spray, saving money and doing a better job.

Nature is brilliant and children seem to sense its brilliance instinctively. They participate in it directly. When you were a kid you imitated your favorite animals, collected flowers, dove into piles of raked leaves, chased butterflies, and acted like a monkey. This behavior, in a way, was your first venture into metaphorical thinking. It was like looking at nature's paper.

When a child imitates a dog, for example, the kid gets a peek at a whole new point of view. What it's like to move on all fours, to bark, and maybe even a little of the frustration, like running into table legs or trying to communicate with just a few, crude sounds. I don't doubt for a second that anyone who imitates a dog fails to gain a better appreciation for the value of the spoken word. No lecture by any parent or teacher can possibly drive the message home more effectively. And you can be sure it gets written into their DNA.

Studying nature will make you marvel. Then you can steal from it like Leonardo da Vinci, who designed musical pipes based on the structure of the human larynx, or Philo Farnsworth, who stole the idea for his television picture tube from the neat rows of crops in a nearby farm in Idaho. Many scientists realize that Mother Nature has solved just about any problem they'll come across. And if you look hard and long enough, you can find a problem nature has solved that is similar enough to your problem to give you a similar solution.

Sometimes you have to look real close. A pair of British scientists noticed that a desert beetle manages to collect precious water from fog. They carefully examined the insect's back under an electron microscope and saw an arrangement of bumps where fog condenses into water and tiny valleys where the water runs to the bug's mouth. Could someone imitate this natural invention and help reduce fog where it's dangerous or collect water where it's scarce? In order to prevent rust, automobile makers already build in channels that direct the flow of water from the roof of the car out the bottom of the frame.

CHALLENGE	SEE	SAW	RESULT
Prevent rust	Beetle's tiny water channels	Trip to the Zoo	Automotive water drainage

Did nature inspire these improvements in water removal systems? Of course! There's literally no limit to the solutions you can steal from nature. But you've got to get in there. Dr. Campbell crawled around in guano in bat caves to figure out what kind of roost would attract bats. You've got to look with wonder and appreciation. Kids are natural naturalists, so naturally they get more out of nature. You can, too, when you think like a kid about how to apply nature's solution to your problem. What problems are on your mind right now? Reduce the description of your problem to one sentence. Now with that sentence, find some strategic stimulation that nature can provide you.

THE CULO COOLER

When I was young my family would go on cross-country road trips from Cincinnati to places like the Grand Tetons, Yellowstone, and the Badlands of South Dakota. Before we owned a car with air conditioning, the rides were always grueling. My father, the inventor, would often complain that his tush got unbearably hot. Back in the '60s, driving around without air conditioning made for a sweaty ride. Open windows cooled you some but not your butt or your back.

So my dad devised a system to cool his butt—the Culo Cooler (*Culo* means "butt" in Italian). He rigged up a plexiglass air scoop fastened to the upper edge of the driver's side window with a hose going into a hollowed-out pillow beneath his tush. It worked! When our car reached cruising speeds of 60 MPH or more, my father's derriere remained cool and refreshed.

The invention, however, had its bugs. Literally. As we drove through regions with high concentrations of flying insects, the Culo Cooler would violently force stunned bugs along with cool, refreshing air into the pillow under my dad's road weary rump. Maybe that explains why he always had a bug up his ass.

SQUARE PEG, ROUND HOLE

When we're trying to solve a problem, too often we go to the same source for help. No wonder we get the same old kinds of solutions. Instead of putting the round peg in the round hole, remember how nature works—randomly and chaotically. At the chaotic center of our galaxy at this very minute, great masses of stars are forming, dying, and blowing debris far into space. It's a mess. But it's our home and we love it.

Why not put those wildly random forces behind the way you

think? Try putting the square peg in the round hole. You did when you were a kid. Unfortunately school taught you to settle for the obvious. So when faced with a problem, you probably looked for an organized problem-solving method. You may have used some, and some of them worked, but in spite of themselves. They seem to work when the people who use them work their butts off, deadline looming, and bump into a solution out of sheer determination and perseverance.

The secret to cheating in idea generation is to color outside the lines.

We've all been hardwired to think that certain things belong together and other things don't. (Ever play that game as a kid where you have to find the object in the picture that doesn't belong?) And yet a quick review of creative breakthroughs shows that every one is a combination of at least two previously unrelated ideas.

> All things can somehow be linked together either in a physical, psychological, or symbolic way.
>
> – UCKMINSTER FULLER

Sometimes the breakthrough gets the name of the word combination as in "horseless carriage" for car or "thinking machine" for computer. Sometimes the combination is hidden in another language as in "democracy," which means "government by the people," literally "people power." Or "karate," meaning "empty hand."

Imagine the reaction to some of these combinations. Karate. "Let me get this straight. You want to teach me how to fight without weapons?" Democracy. "What? Are you nuts? Put the people in charge of themselves!" Horseless carriage. "Where the heck do we hang the feedbag?"

Obviously it takes some naked thinking to recognize the beauty of an idea while it still appears to be ridiculous. To a kid an "arm clock" might make perfect sense. To an adult who grew up with "a clock is the huge piece of furniture standing in the hallway," it might take more mental energy. Pretend that the innovations listed below came from the idea combinations next to them. Try to imagine how odd they may have seemed before they won acceptance. Then imagine how to get from the crazy combination to the working result.

IDEA COMBINATION	BREAKTHROUGH
Arm clock	Wristwatch
Words on paper	Book
Electric candle	Light bulb
Share property	Communism
Indoor outhouse	Bathroom

In most cases a lot of different combinations could have inspired these breakthroughs, but in every case it took vision and courage to follow the idea down to its creation. A child will force-fit things with no apparent relationship. They don't know any better. (Is that better or worse?) Have you ever heard a kid sing a song, whether or not they know the words? We all could use more of that open-minded, on-the-fly thinking. So let's practice.

EXERCISE
Combinations

Randomly pick a word from Column A and another from Column B. Make the combination work as one of the following:

1. Plot for a Movie

2. Children's candy

3. Theme for a party

4. The perfect gift

COLUMN A	COMBINATION	COLUMN B
Morph		Skin
Underwater		House
Eliminate		Dog
Carry		Pencil
Green		Society
Portable		Flower
Invisible		Airplane
Fast		Bed
Odorless		Soup

Don't stop. Don't limit yourself to my four kinds of results. Take the combination wherever it leads you. Brain chain. Then make more lists. Get some other DNA into play. When you're ready to work on a real problem, put some thought behind your lists. One list should incorporate as many of the facets of the current product or situation as possible. The other should contain all manner of words that might relate to where you want to be or what you want to happen and then some. Add some unconnected, randomly selected words, too.

ROUND BALL, ROUND HOLE

The principal problem with putting the round peg in the round hole is no change. The peg doesn't change. The hole stays the same. When there's no change, nothing happens. When nothing happens, it's not worth talking about. Yawn! I learned this lesson cleaning my dad's tool-and-dye shop one afternoon. Actually I didn't learn the lesson until many years later, because nothing happened until I started looking for lessons in everyday events.

One day my dad asked me to clean up his shop. I was busy sweeping up metal shavings when I noticed some cool ball bearings on his bench. I set the broom aside (I could get to that later) and started putzing around with a ball bearing. Suddenly the round-peg-round-hole syndrome overcame me. I absolutely had to find out where the ball bearing would fit. The drill press, of course. There were holes all around the chuck. (That's the cylinder that holds the drill bit in place. The holes are for the key that tightens the chuck. It's called the chuck key. Sometimes it gets gummed up with what machinists call "chuck-key cheese." Just kidding!)

Anyway, I popped the ball bearing into the hole. It fit perfectly. The problem was, I couldn't get it out. And it's still in that hole today. A constant reminder that, yes, just because things fit perfectly doesn't mean they're meant to be.

APPLYING STRATEGIC STIMULATION

First, has the problem been solved by somebody else already? Do your research. Go to your DNA chart and ask the appropriate source how they would solve the problem. Understand the best work done to date. If you don't find a satisfactory solution, then it's time to apply strategic stimulation.

For example, let's say your screen door slams. Too much noise, you hate it. There's a very simple solution to your problem. Visit your local hardware store and tell one of the staff your problem. Chances are you'll get fixed up with a simple, pneumatic device that you screw to the door and the jamb. No more slamming door.

Okay, but what if the standard solution doesn't satisfy you? Maybe you want a less installation fuss or simpler technology. Maybe you don't want to spend $20 or don't have the time to do anything but fix it now with whatever you've got on hand around your house. Now you face the kind of challenge that makes naked thinking worthwhile.

In this *challenge*, as always, you have a number of resources, abilities, information, and skills at your disposal—what you See. Now you want to look at the challenge the way you Saw things as a child. So you playfully wander around, looking at stuff, you've got. Maybe something inspires you. Maybe not. Then you study the door and notice it has a force when it closes. If you hang something from the door handle, it swings out when the door closes. Suddenly you realize that if something were attached loosely to the door, something that would end up between the door and the jamb at just the right moment, something soft... Voila! Result.

After a bit of experimentation, you hang a tennis ball on a short length of twine on the inside of the door near the edge that opens. When the door swings closed, the ball swings out, gets caught between the door and jamb, takes the force of the slamming door, and mutes the sound of the slam. Then it conveniently rolls out of the way allowing the door to close quietly.

CHALLENGE	SEE	SAW	RESULT
Prevent door from slamming	Tennis ball, twine, nail, or screw	Let the Force Be with You	Swinging-ball door-slam suppressor

I've simplified and narrowed down the elements of the process so you can see what really matters—the balance between your adult experience and your childlike, playful way of looking at things. You could have come up with any number of solutions, using any of the Think Naked techniques. And you should play and practice all of them, all the time. The more you do, the more surprisingly novel solutions you'll encounter.

UBERKID

Talent favors repetition. So if you want some talent, practice. Live it, love it. Stick with it like a kid learning how to slide into second base, perfecting a cheerleading move or a difficult passage on the piano, or repeating the Barney "I Love You" song everywhere they go.

Any athlete or musician will vouch for the value of practice. Coming out of a concert, you sometimes hear someone say, "I wish I could play like that." As if the performer were born with the ability to dazzle. No! It takes practice. Practice to the point of exhaustion. An effective weightlifting tactic involves what are known as forced repetitions—movements that are not quite complete or proper but force the muscle to a new point of exhaustion. This leaves the muscle in a position to grow stronger with the proper rest and nourishment. The same goes for practicing your Think Naked exercises. Practice. Practice. Practice. And then practice some more.

Think of practice as cheating. Don't think of it as work. Even though it may be difficult, even painful, you're doing what you like. So enjoy what you're doing. Keep reminding yourself that you're getting better, but don't concentrate on getting better. You won't notice it if you watch for it. Think about what you're doing. Let getting better come as a free gift. Let your progress surprise you.

And don't forget to practice everything. Continue to fend off fear using the "Wear Your Cape" principles. Keep your cape advantages up to date. Practice the blockbusters in the previous chapter. Do something to push yourself a little further every day. Get good at the cheating exercises you've learned in this chapter. Make them a habit. When you're secure in your cape, busting blocks as easily as you sneeze, cheating every chance you get, you'll be ready for the next dimension of the Think Naked way of life—"Show-N-Tell."

7

SHOW-N-TELL

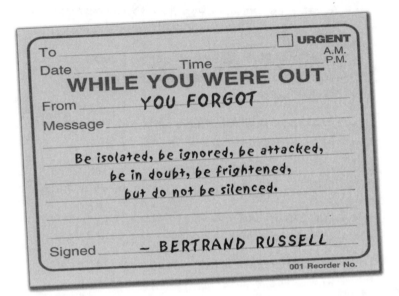

To _____
Date _____ Time _____
WHILE YOU WERE OUT
From _____ *YOU FORGOT* _____
Message _____

Be isolated, be ignored, be attacked,
be in doubt, be frightened,
but do not be silenced.

— BERTRAND RUSSELL

Signed _____

☐ **URGENT**
A.M.
P.M.

001 Reorder No.

This chapter is divided into three sections: Show, Tell, and Listen, plus some important concluding advice. The sections hold 13 Think Naked techniques that will take you from just thinking naked to putting your naked thinking into practice. The final step on your way to a life free of despair.

- *I WANNA BE A FIREFIGHTER* kicks off the Pure Intent section with a look at what you really want to be and to do with your life.

- *HIGH CONCEPT* introduces the idea of developing your life's mantra, using mine as an example.

- **BLUE SUNS, YELLOW SKIES** opens the Show section by showing you how to express yourself in pictures—from drawings to doodles.

- **NAKED BARBIE** gives you permission to express all of life's natural drives, including sex.

- **PLAY-DOH POSSIBILITIES** points out the benefits of expressing yourself in 3-D.

- **NO SHAME IN YOUR GAME** starts the Tell section with permission to say what's on your mind.

- **FOR CRYIN' OUT LOUD!** promotes the wisdom of taking action whenever it's called for.

- **REPEAT OFFENDER** encourages you to speak out without filtering your thoughts.

- **CUT TO THE CHASE** eliminates the need to hedge when it comes to expressing yourself.

- **MILK, MILK, LEMONADE** introduces the benefits of using humor when dealing with taboo subject matter.

- **HABLA BLAH-BLAH** encourages the free and uninhibited invention of language as needed.

- **TELL ME A STORY** offers some tips on the skill of elaboration.

- **POR FAVOR, SAY SOME MORE,** the only principle of the Listen section, promotes empathy and advantages of hearing what others have to say.

The techniques conclude with a look at your Embarrassment Threshold, how to raise it, and the powerful practice of Engage and Distribute.

Two African American sprinters stand on the medal podium with heads bowed and fists raised at the Mexico City Games in 1968. Not only one of the most memorable moments in Olympic history but a milestone in America's civil rights movement.

The dominant figure, Tommie Smith, son of a poor Texas sharecropper, expressed himself only when pushed. He had learned to stifle his rage against the constant humiliation his family suffered kowtowing to their landowner. But today it would be different. He had just earned his way to the top of an international forum. The fastest man on earth was about to deliver a message.

Tommie and other black Olympic athletes had decided to protest the inequality African Americans still suffered nearly two hundred years after the Declaration of Independence declared that "all men are created equal." Some wanted to boycott the games. Throughout his childhood Tommie had always wanted the world to know how intensely he resented the plight of American blacks. But a boycott wouldn't do. He had walked away too often. Better to give the world his best, he thought, and then deliver his message.

The athletes agreed they would all protest in their own way. They would remind America that its civil rights movement had not gone far enough to eliminate the injustices systematically heaped on black Americans. Smith called his wife and they contemplated how he would express himself. Then he and teammate John Carlos secretly planned a non-violent protest in the manner of Martin Luther King Jr. In the 200-meter race, Smith won the gold medal and Carlos the bronze. The world was watching.

The lean, handsome, six-foot-four-inch black man stands straight and proud on the summit of the three-stepped winners' stand. The stadium, packed with admiring fans, waits. A champion should be high on the wings of victory, but Smith remains somber. No, quietly defiant. In what should be his moment of celebration, he possesses the calm determination of someone with a mission. As the opening notes of his national anthem ring through the stadium, Tommie Smith bows his head and thrusts his right, gloved fist like a ramrod at the sky.

As the final strains of the anthem play and voices raise the words, "land of the free, home of the brave," Tommie lowers his fist, executes a military about-face, and steps away. Stunned white America gets the message, loud and clear. With the rest of the world they have watched another courageous African American with the pure intent of Rosa Parks say, "Enough! No more back of the bus. No more second class treatment."

Smith later told reporters that he raised his right, black-gloved fist to represent black power in America. John Carlos' left fist also gloved in black, represented unity in black America. Together they formed an arch of unity and power. The black scarf around Smith's neck stood for black pride. Their shoeless feet in black socks represented black poverty in racist America. My friend Tommie confided to me, "I took the stand my way. It was my moment and I wasn't going to salute a flag that didn't recognize me as a man, as a human being."

While the Mexico City protest seems relatively tame by today's standards, the actions of Smith and Carlos were met with outrage. Both were suspended from their national team and banned from the Olympic Village, the athletes' home during the games. It seems white America could handle Rosa Parks, a mild-mannered black woman. But when the model of black manhood, the epitome of speed and strength got out of line, whites recoiled in fear and hatred. A few supporters praised Smith and Carlos for their bravery, but most cried out against what they called militant behavior that disgraced Americans. The backlash brought death threats against both men and their families. When asked if he would do it again, Tommie replied, "I do it every day."

You, too, need to express yourself every day. That's the intent of this chapter. It will give you tools for unleashing the four-year-old who has just discovered the treasure trove of your wonderful life. What you do with this powerful combination is entirely up to you. You don't have to affect the world the way Tommie Smith, Picasso, Betty Friedan, Isaac Newton, or Abraham Lincoln did. But you may.

We're going to look at the intentions that guide you and how to clarify and purify them. Then I'm going to ask you to find what makes you passionate, to express that passion in a High Concept, nail it to your wall, and put it into practice. I'll present practical exercises in two parts—Show and Tell. Then I'll wrap up the chapter with a section called Listen. It's all about empathy. It will help you balance what you express with sensitivity to what those around you need.

I'm going to recommend a lot of things you already do. But please don't gloss over them. Just as a yoga teacher shows you how to breathe more effectively, I'm going to show you how to be more aware of how you express yourself today and how to get more out of expression tomorrow.

WHEN I GROW UP

What do you want to be when you grow up? Have you asked yourself that question lately? Do you ever have to grow up? Does growing up mean you've arrived? What is it to feel like when you've arrived? Have you? Arrived, that is?

A healthy bit of commitment to a stated goal makes the road you're on feel more mapped out, even if your map is nothing more than an intended destination. When I told my parents I was writing a book, I got a "That's nice, son" comment from my mother. You see, we have a long family history of big talk in our family. I knew I had to deliver this time or my word would not be worth as much down the road. So I was bound and determined to finish. I also remember the commitment I had prior to stating it out loud.

Along the way Marco Polo Explorers has improved, thanks to the research needed for this book. I've made a ton of contacts at the speeches I get to do around the country, and now that you're reading this, you know I was true to my word.

But when I reflect on the thought of charting a course (finishing a book) I never realize how the journey will change me more profoundly than actually reaching the end goal. Sometimes knowing you've arrived only happens after you reflect on the way you navigated your way there.

So what do you want to do? What's your intended destination? What do you hope to learn on the way? What do you want to do when you grow up?

I WANNA BE A FIREFIGHTER

I Wanna Be a Firefighter, ballerina, doctor, mountain climber, truck driver, junk dealer. Ask a child what they want to be when they grow up. Not only will they tell you, they'll act out that dream in the way they look, dress, and act. The little firefighter knows he has to be aggressive and decisive. The ballerina tries to solve problems with elegance, poise, and serenity.

Most of us have already decided what we want to be, what we want to do with our lives. Okay, maybe you've changed your mind any number of times, but you know what excites you, what you like to do. Now it's time to put real passion behind your inclinations or new fire underneath the dream you want to pursue with greater passion. To do that, it helps to write and rely on a High Concept.

I Wanna Be a Firefighter is a kid version of a High Concept. And it works. By trying to understand how a firefighter would handle things, a child gets an idea of how to act. Kids who stick to an original plan learn more and more every day how to be what they plan to be. It's so rare, though, for a kid to maintain his or her original dream. Bombarded with so many attractive possibilities, they typically jump from one to the other. They see a doctor save a bird with a broken wing on TV, "I wanna be a veterinarian!" Typically a pattern develops, though. If a kid wants to be a vet, for example, most of that kid's play involves animals and caring. In this kind of pattern lies what I call a High Concept.

Whether you realize it or not, your best thoughts, finest ideas, and purest motives stem from a simple, focused theme. Your job is to find that theme. People with strong, religious guidance personify a theme in their God. Members and fans of athletic teams embrace and are driven by the team's colors, logos, mascot, and fight song. You can make your entire life shine with one, central purpose that directs every day. Like other highly motivated individuals, you need to clearly identify and articulate your High Concept. Call it your core mission, your mantra, or your roadmap, but state it briefly in a short phrase or with a few words. It works. You'll be amazed at how much falls into place after you complete this step.

When you know what you want to be and you state it out loud, your next steps become clear. Deciding what to do in any circumstance becomes easier when you can easily refer to your stated will. Like the kid who has always dreamed about being a firefighter, you live for wearing the slick jacket, sliding down the pole, and saving lives under the wail of the siren with a Dalmatian by your side. It's all about aspiration. Less important are how you're perceived and how much money you make.

HIGH CONCEPT

So what do you want to be? What are the words that will drive you there? This collection of words should be easy to remember, distinctly yours, actionable, and result oriented. I'll explain all that, but first, use my High Concept as an example as we walk through how to write yours.

STEP 1

Flip through your favorite magazines and find images that say something about you. Look for people, places, and things you identify with. With the images in front of you, come up with a list of words that the images bring to mind. Then look over your list of words and choose one or two words that summarize the list.

In my case, this exercise identified the unifying theme of my actions. Something common to everything I did. I've always been an obstinate SOB; poking holes in phony ideas, lashing out at unjust practices, never in love with rules or rule makers for that matter, and always believing that there was a better way and that I could find it. Defiant sounds like a word you'd use to describe me, wouldn't you say?

My result: DEFIANCE

STEP 2

Name famous and everyday people you know whom you admire. List the defining traits of these people. How would you describe each of them in a word or two? After you've made an exhaustive list, look for recurring words and themes. Find the words that best describe you or what you'd like to be. Nothing impossible, though. The words ought to describe things you've done or moments in your life that were driven by the words. Once again, look over your list of words and choose one or two words that summarize them.

As an example, here are the lists I developed for myself. I named three leading characters from movies and a basketball star. Then I listed words and phrases that described their characters.

SPARTACUS

Idealism
Purpose
In the trenches
Defiant
Fighter for fairness
Trying to make things better

SHANE

Integrity
Good at what he did
Fought for the underdog
Had a positive impact
Honorable

COOL HAND LUKE

Defiant
Giver of Hope
Irrepressible
Thinker
Stubborn

BILL RUSSELL

Against the grain
Fought for black rights
Innovator
Not pleased with the status quo
A team player

These people personify the goals and dreams I want to fulfill. I see a common theme. It has to do with rebellion, but rebellion with a purpose. It comes from my idealism, which I may have more of than I need. Since I have a finite amount of energy and can't apply my idealism against every injustice, stupid practice, and ridiculous rule, I've decided to pick my battles. You could say I've become more purposeful. Okay, now I've got half of my High Concept—Purposeful Defiance. The words are actionable. They describe something I can do. And they're directed. They tell me how to do it.

My result: PURPOSEFUL DEFIANCE

STEP 3

Now all you have to do is balance the second half of your High Concept with action and results. Then make the words fit together. There's no future in creating a High Concept you can't live up to, so find words that describe what you can do. Decide whom and what you want your action to affect. Describe clearly the results you want to achieve. In short, make your High Concept actionable, directed, result oriented, and based on your proven momentum. If you want to ice the cake, make them rhyme or sound catchier. This will help endear them to you.

I've always felt that my ultimate goal in life is to create something good and lasting. I need to direct the majority of my energy towards creating something positive or else I slip into the dumps. I have a wonderful son and try to respect and nurture him in his development. My company, Marco Polo Explorers, helps companies create new products and services. We help reposition tired, old brands. We help promote and enliven some of the greatest brands on the planet. By writing books, I want to share what I've discovered in years of research—that we all have it in us to create an incredible life. The charities I support help children. So the second, result-oriented half of my High Concept becomes Positive Impact.

My High Concept:
PURPOSEFUL DEFIANCE, POSITIVE IMPACT

In my case, Purposeful Defiance is balanced by Positive Impact. One side of the equation reflects how I look at things and approach a situation and the other represents the intended goal. Purposeful Defiance, Positive Impact. I print it on the back of my business cards. I state it as the Marco Polo Explorers company mission. I use it to direct myself minute by minute. My High Concept has become the way I see and guide my life.

I've shown you mine; now show me yours. You will want to take some time with this. Go away somewhere. Don't rush it. Of course, you will want to talk to the people closest to you. You may find some very interesting insights about yourself. Some of the qualities you think shine through in you may not shine as brightly as you think. At the same time, you may find that your loved ones find greater qualities you had no idea you possessed.

ORNITHOPHOBIA

The producers of *The View* asked me to come on their national TV show and help one of the cohosts create her High Concept in a live, eight-minute segment. Did that sound ridiculous as I described it? Well, it should. It takes some people their whole adult lives to create a High Concept. I'm going to do it in eight minutes?

To further complicate things, after we found her High Concept, we planned to help her with a specific phobia, in order to prove that my method of strategic problem solving actually worked.

She was afraid of birds, ornithophobia. A woodpecker had attacked her at the age of seven and she'd never been able to shake her fear of birds.

Here's what I did. First, I asked her to react to some nature pictures. I wanted her to pick the pictures that she most identified with and to tell me why. She picked a crashing wave and said that she identified with it because she was aggressive and tense. She picked a peacock, because she was proud, confident, and knowledgeable.

After looking at a number of pictures, the words *aggressive* and *confident* recurred enough that we decided they should be part of her High Concept. If we had had the time, we would have written the words *aggressive* and *confident* into an actionable statement and added a result-oriented second half of her High Concept. But now it was time to see if the two words we had identified could help her overcome her fear of birds.

What would be a confident and aggressive approach to dealing with her phobia? Bring a bird out on stage. That's what we did. Would she handle the bird with confidence or run away screaming? With two minutes left, she met the bird. She was tense, but with 30 seconds left, she was petting the bird with confidence. This may sound boastful, but I doubt she would have done so without having been introduced to her High Concept, such as it was.

SUPPRESS OR EXPRESS

We all express ourselves. Not always as dramatically as Tommie Smith, but we do express. We can improve the way we express and learn to express more, but first we have to understand why and how we suppress. It makes good sense to hold your tongue sometimes. I can't tell you how many times I've been told that. At the same time, we can't

> No person is your friend who demands your silence or denies your right to grow.
>
> — ALICE WALKER

always tell the truth. Watch Jim Carrey in *Liar, Liar* if you think total honesty is always the best policy. Rather than lie or be perfectly honest, we wisely choose to suppress—keep our mouths shut in some situations. So far so good. These are reasonable excuses for suppressing.

However, as we learned in Chapters 2 and 3, we also suppress our feelings and ideas out of fear. We learned how we've been taught to suppress our instincts and intuition. Getting "The Look" time and time again teaches us to suppress. As you might suspect, all this suppression works against thinking naked. Not good. Both are bad excuses for suppressing.

The more you think naked—protected by your cape, handily blockbusting, cheating as much as possible—the more you feel like expressing yourself. You shout when you're happy. You kick your heels. Less afraid, you say more often what you feel. You let people know when you're angry with them. With more hardwired blocks busted, you start acting more like a kid with the coolest new toy than an adult numbed by the sameness of routine. You begin to experience things on a more visceral level. Everything feels so much more honest.

In short, you develop passion. Passion gives permission. You become less inclined to deny yourself, more expressive. That doesn't mean you just talk, laugh, and cry louder and more often. When you turn your four-year-old loose on all the information you've gathered in your adult life, you come up with more and better ways to express. Your family, community, school, or business benefits from your new ability to express.

SHOW

Loss of passion might easily rank as the most common and devastating disease of modern adulthood. It sure seems to me that a heck of a lot of people drag their butts through life. Doing what they have to do rather than what they want to do. That's not exactly a statistically verifiable fact, but I'm gonna go with my gut. That's what the *Show* part of this chapter is all about—going with your gut. Being true to the amazing exuberance that I'm betting you've suppressed since childhood. The little genius in you who enabled you to run around the house, smash your cookies with your mom's shoe, draw on the side-walk, eat with the dog, and leap into rain puddles.

> The masses of men lead lives of quiet desperation.
>
> – HENRY DAVID THOREAU

Before we get into the techniques, I'd like you to find a favorite picture of your-self as a child. Look at your eyes. Look at that expression! That was you! That screwy fun, goofy, excited-about-life little person was you. You were brilliant. This first group of Show techniques will help you go with that kid's gut. They will help you let your childlike pas-sions you see in those eyes drive your adult life.

As soon as you let that kid take your adult life experience and run with it, you'll never be the same. With your experience and that kid's genius, you'll be formidable. Just don't let the adult run the child. Don't stifle the naked thinking you. Use your infor-mation, but honor the kid's impulses. You'll never feel the despair of being in a hole with no way out. You'll know it's not a hole but the beginning of a tunnel to China or a chance to make friends with a groundhog and have him lead you to a gold deposit where Spiderman waits to help you use it for the good of the human race.

BLUE SUNS, YELLOW SKIES

At some point in your life you made your first attempt to represent the world around you. You drew a stick figure of your mom or dad, your house, yourself. To the rest of the world the image probably didn't look a whole lot like your subject. But you knew better. The lines you crayoned were art—a representation, an interpretation of your impressions. That's why you drew a daisy the size of your house—an expression in lines on paper, pure intent in vivid colors. No pretenses. (It took centuries for the world's leading artists to come around to this point of view. And then they had the nerve to call it modern art as if they had just invented it!)

You did what you wanted to do the best way you could. There's great wisdom in that. And if you do it, and keep on doing it, eventually your efforts will bear beautiful results. If you want to express yourself as an artist, cheat by taking in all kinds of art. Stack the deck by using the best materials. Or not. With your adult wealth of experience, you'll express even better than you did as a kid as long as you put your four-year-old genius in charge.

EXERCISE
Draw Me a Picture

Get a blank piece of paper and a pencil. Take a minute to relax, and then try to draw without planning a picture. Think about what you want to draw and start making bold marks on the page. Don't judge the results. Just enjoy yourself. If you don't like what you see, start over. Stick with this exercise for ten minutes or more. If you draw just for the fun of it, you'll love the results. Why not display your favorite effort on the refrigerator?

Why limit yourself to paper? You can carry the same kidlike expression into the rest of your world. What about the way you dress, the way you decorate your room, apartment, or home—your Happy Place? You can hang fuzzy dice from your rearview mirror if you want to. Chartreuse ones. You can wear a pinstriped suit with dreadlocks. Construct a huge crib in your bedroom with a waterbed mattress. Hang furniture from the ceiling or go completely the other way and make your house look like a cathedral or a barn.

Just don't forget to cheat. Look at Architectural Digest. The more you cheat, the more you'll see that a lot of cutting edge artists, decorators, musicians, designers and the like have already captured what you want to express. That's what they do. Buy their stuff. Use the force they've already created and improve it. Make your environment—from what you wear to where you live and work—as much an expression of you as possible.

Make room for your personal interpretations in every corner of your life. Like the child who represents something that does not exist, entertain possibilities you've never considered. Choose colors, scents, sounds, and flavors just because they appeal to you— especially if it goes against the accepted way of doing things in your world.

STICK MAN, FINGER PAINT

With adults it seems everything ends up in words. It's difficult for some people to understand that Beethoven's *Symphony No. 5* says something. We don't need someone to come along and explain what it says in words. It says much more than words can express. Otherwise Ludwig might have scratched out an essay instead. He didn't just say something bigger and more loudly. He expressed something words couldn't touch. Watch Edward G. Robinson in the movie, *Soylent Green*. He liked the "Fifth" so much he used it as his exit-from-the-world music.

The same goes for Pablo Picasso, Martha Graham, Igor Stravinsky, Auguste Rodin, and Annie Leibowitz. Painting, dance, music, sculpture, and photography all express ideas that leave words wanting. Why else would dictators and religious fanatics work so ruthlessly to ban them?

When words and letters were still practically meaningless to you, you expressed yourself in crude and simple images. Drawing remains a great way to express yourself. Psychologists understand that drawings may express more than your words can. A symbol can convey an entire thought in one image. Some languages rely entirely on iconic symbols. Notice how common icons have become in computer programs, chat rooms, and e-mail messages.

It's time you got back to doodling if you've ever stopped. Doodling as a form of symbolic expression could be a great way to start loosening up your visual expression skills. But don't stop there. Get in the habit of doodling when you're on the phone or in a meeting. When you're not consciously focused on a problem, your subconscious works on it and can express itself through your doodles. Play Pictionary. Become a graffiti artist. Next time you present an idea at work, use illustrations or pictures to communicate your thoughts. Get out of the word rut and you'll find yourself understanding and expressing more than you ever imagined.

HIGH FINANCE

Okay, I'm not a math genius. So when I sat down with my accountant one time and tried to explain what I wanted, it was too number complicated for me to express. So I drew her this diagram:

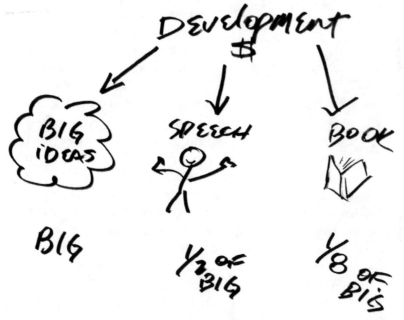

I said, "I want this much from here to go over here, so that this pile gets this big."

When I draw her a picture, I don't have to do numbers. And I don't have to use words I don't really understand. It's dangerous to use words you don't understand. You're bound to be misunderstood.

When she talks about *appreciation* and *closely held*, I'm thinking one thing and I know she's thinking something else. When she uses words like *top down* and *convertible*, I know we're talking different languages. And when she gets into *non-discretionary accrual, debenture, FIFO, subvention, accretion,* and *derivatives,* I'm still cruising around in the convertible.

NAKED BARBIE

Okay, time to face it. You're no longer innocent. You lost it a long time ago. Maybe it was the time you saw someone naked and

> When I conceived Barbie, I believed it was important to a little girl's self-esteem to play with a doll that has breasts.
>
> – RUTH HANDLER

realized, "Uh-oh, I'm interested in a different way!" Sex has made its way into your life and your life has changed forever. Welcome to the club. We humans are so sexual and so preoccupied with sex that we try to ignore it just to get something else done. We suppress our thoughts about sex, limit our discussion of it, and try to lock it in the closet. And it never works.

Sexual curiosity drives so much creativity, invention, and exploration that they should teach it to product development teams in corporate R&D departments. The obvious examples of our preoccupation with sex hits us in the face every day. Real geniuses, however, create fame and fortune by pushing the borders of sexual expression in subtler, more graceful ways. The way Ruth Handler did in 1959. When it was all but inconceivable to even think of letting little girls own a doll with breasts, she introduced the Barbie doll.

Some adults of her day, comfortable with the conservative tone of the '50s, refused to let their daughters own Barbie dolls. But no one could stem the tide of hundreds and thousands of girls who clamored for Barbie. Throughout her lifetime, Barbie has weathered a variety of assaults and continues to thrive. All because Ruth Handler sensed it was important for girls to imagine what they might like to be. Her hunch, based on watching her daughter play with paper dolls, required her to break a sexual taboo. When she did, she opened up a wonderful world of imagination for countless numbers of young girls. Barbie has become nearly essential to the formation a young girl's self-image.

Children automatically do things they're not supposed to. When an adult says, "Don't do that," a child seems to sense it must be worth doing. How many inventors, athletes, and business people become more determined to succeed when told, "It can't be done?" This tells me that if you want to bring exciting, new opportunities into your life, you may have to venture into something just on the edge of forbidden. Something forbidden that really shouldn't be forbidden. Sometimes you have to do what you've been told couldn't be done.

What are some of the untouchable, unbreakable hurdles you face? The Barbies you really want to show the world, but you haven't, because you're afraid. It's normal to fear rejection and embarrassment. But for some of us the thing we really need to do just happens to be outside the lines. And when it comes to our happiness, we have little choice but to do it.

PLAY-DOH POSSIBILITIES

Let's say you're having a house built. What would you rather see: blueprints, drawings, or a 3-D model? Each has its value, but the model allows you to more easily put yourself into the idea of the house. If three contractors came to you—one with blueprints, one with drawings and photographs, and another with a model or even a virtual video tour of the proposed plan—you'd probably feel most comfortable with the model maker, if only because the model demonstrates the contractor's total immersion in the work.

If a picture is worth a thousand words, a great prototype is worth millions. Make that a trillion, because you can take it in, not just with your eyes, but also with your hands, nose, and ears. Who better understands what a snake is all about, the kid who describes one, the kid who draws one, or the kid who makes one out of clay? You've rolled clay in your hands. You know you get an understanding of the snake shape no picture can match.

The more dimensions you put into the expression of your ideas, the richer and more alive your ideas will be. Along the way in the making of your prototype, you'll force yourself to answer many questions and make important decisions. You have to make real parts of your idea that pictures and words can fudge. You and your audience will both benefit from your effort.

TELL

Speech comes so natural to most of us. We learn to speak, develop the foundation of our vocabulary, manage basic grammar and syntax, and color our language with accent and inflection before we reach age three. It should come as no surprise then to think of language as a kid thing.

> In the beginner's mind there are many possibilities; in the expert's mind there are few.
>
> — SHUNRYU SUZUKI

In his book, *The Monkey in the Mirror*, Ian Tattersall suggests that children may have invented language. Or in his words, "it is not implausible that a rudimentary precursor of language as it is familiar today initially arose in a group of children, in the context of play." Didn't we just say the same thing? Yes but not the same way. I'm writing to you and Ian is writing to the scientific community. Let me tell you why this is so important. I want to do two things:

1. Encourage you to express yourself in words

2. Show you how to tune your language to your audience and the situation

Wait. Let's not gloss over Ian's amazing claim. Children invented language! Makes sense, doesn't it? Little cave dudes probably started tagging their parents and their parents' uncool friends with different sounds. Maybe some sound associated with the person. When grumpy Uncle Gork came into the cave they'd make a grump sound and laugh. I'm sure the adults were clueless for the longest time. And when they finally figured out what was going on, no doubt they tried to put an end to it.

When Ian Tattersall talks about this, he cites a study of macaque monkeys on a Japanese island that were fed sweet potatoes by researchers.

These delicacies became covered with beach grit, and pretty soon, young macaques started washing them in the sea to remove the sand. It took a while for the adults to catch on: first the females, and only last the dominant males. Doubtless, some of the older and most dominant males never deigned to indulge in this behavior, preferring a familiar life of grit.

When you consider how adults balk at every new form of expression that emerges from youth culture—jazz, rock-n-roll, beat poetry, rap—it's fun to imagine our cave dwelling ancestors trying to rail against language itself. Funnier still when you keep in mind they lacked the words to do so. Do I need to say anything else to make my point about thinking like a butt-naked kid?

No SHAME IN YOUR GAME

Swishing around in the bathtub, the little boy stops and exclaims, "Look, Daddy, now it's like a pencil!" Gulp! Okay, we're not supposed to talk about erections and stuff like that in mixed company. But it's funny. It feels good to laugh about a child's innocent self-discovery. How can it be bad? It's not. It's pure. And that's the first step in learning how to express yourself in words. You have to believe with a clear heart that what you think and feel deserves no shame.

Clarification: Yes, if you're a creep and you talk about sex to embarrass, to insult, to overpower, or to titillate people when it's not appropriate, you should be ashamed of yourself. But when you're working from childlike pure intent, you can and you will say what your gut feels.

Think back to those incredible moments of discovery you enjoyed as a kid. Remember how your reactions came straight from your gut? It felt great! Then one of your innocent "Aha!" moments drew a response from the genius-geek kid, "Duh! Everybody knows that." From then on you began to stifle your gut response. Now as an adult you might squelch any urge to express wonder. You might be too embarrassed to marvel at Tchaikovsky's *1812 Overture* for fear some weathered classical music aficionado will overhear you and scoff with a pompous yawn, "I must say I've grown rah-ther weary of that particular warhorse."

Hey! Are you crapping me? Tchaikovsky was great! Have no shame in your game. You are where you are on your life's road and you can't be anywhere else. So why pretend? Go ahead and do what you like to do without feeling embarrassed. Sing out loud. Who cares if you suck? You'll feel better. Eat dessert first. Yodel in the library. Shake yourself up and you'll shake things up and create a safer environment for thinking naked. Train yourself to listen for your gut response instead of the rehearsed or edited version. Your gut will tell you what to say and write. Trust it even when your adult censor raises its eyebrows.

THE DUMB BAR

When you know you can't possibly look dumber than the guy who just said the dumbest thing you've ever heard, you tend to get a safe, cushy feeling. You let yourself go a bit and the inhibitions that once kept you from some freewheeling thoughts are gone.

At Marco Polo Explorers we set the Dumb Bar so high that no one can possibly say anything that will get "The Look" or a dose of ridicule. It's a great way to create comfort in a conversation. Rather than make you look stupid, it disarms you and makes people feel more comfortable with you.

Set your Dumb Bar super high and watch people open up. They say to themselves, "This guy's an idiot. I couldn't possibly say anything more stupid than he just did."

FROM ELLINGTON TO ANDRÉ

The group Outkast has carved out an incredible place in the music industry. In the year 2000, critics tried to categorize them. They weren't funk, hip-hop, or R&B, but you could hear all those influences in their incredibly textural compositions. It was so natural, André 3000, one of the group's front men, attributed their success to thinking naked. "No rules, we just went into the studio and played what sounded good. Instead of wondering what people would think, we did what felt good to us."

When asked how he was able to write so prolifically in such a range of styles, Duke Ellington replied, "Well, I never went to college and learned I couldn't."

FOR CRYIN' OUT LOUD!

Once you've given your gut permission to talk, you might hear some complaints. This is good. Acknowledging there is a problem is the first step towards finding a solution. When babies get hungry they cry. When toddlers tire, they rub their eyes and act all cranky. Children are much better at identifying problems. Most of the time, we aren't as willing to identify problems. You're walking down the hallway at work

> I merely took the energy it takes to pout and wrote some blues.
>
> — DUKE ELLINGTON

feeling sick with the weight of the world on your shoulders. You're friend says, "Hi, how are you?" You say, "Fine. How are you?"

Sometimes we don't realize we have a problem until we finally blow up or lose our temper. A child gets right to the point. "I don't like it!" We can have a gale force temper tantrum raging inside while we talk pleasantly about the weather. Enough of that! When you're sad, cry. When you're angry, let the perpetrator know how you feel. At least admit to yourself that you have a problem. Learn to react to situations and give yourself signals. This will help you admit that there is a problem. Then you can do something about it.

In 1937, Alfred Moen burned his hands when he turned the wrong water handle on the faucet. "The hot water came on sooner than I expected," he reported later. "It got me thinking that you ought to get what you wanted out of a faucet. The more I thought about it, the more I was convinced that a single-handle mixing faucet was the answer, so I began to make some drawings." Instead of gritting his teeth and holding back his anger, Moen acknowledged the problem. Then he did something about it. He expressed it in engineering drawings and words. By 1947 the single-handed faucet hit the market. By 1950, it was a hit. Now they make up more than 70 percent of the kitchen faucets sold in the United States.

CHALLENGE	SEE	SAW	RESULT
Prevent hand burns	Inadequate faucet design	For Cryin' Out Loud	Single-handle mixing faucet

Not all problems get your attention the way they signaled Alfred Moen. Sometimes a feeling of unease kind of sits in your tummy. It might just be a vague sense that something is wrong. Recognize it. Acknowledge it. You'll find it. You certainly won't invent or create anything unless you face the problem. And you won't recognize problems if you stifle your gut reactions.

REPEAT OFFENDER

Once you've acknowledged a problem and expressed out loud what you feel, you can't stop there. Now it's time to say what's on your mind. Maybe I should say, say what's in your gut rather than let your mind filter it. To go beyond, "I don't like that," and make the fullness of your feelings known.

As adults we develop two voices—an out loud voice and a secret voice. Your secret voice is what you're really thinking or feeling. Your out loud voice is what people actually hear you say. We want to avoid giving offense, so we keep our many opinions to ourselves. Using only your secret voice can condemn some great thoughts to a life sentence in solitary confinement, all because we want to stay out of trouble.

Kids still have hearts free of the shame that afflicts and infects so many adults. They still possess purity of intent. They still say exactly what they feel at a given moment—without forethought and without worrying about the consequences. It's their totally unfiltered behavior that surprises and delights unsuspecting listeners. Like when a kid blurts out a perfectly harmless, "I love dawgs!" or "Can I have a rhinoceros for my birthday?" They might also shriek, "Butt crack!" pointing at the refrigerator repairman bent over in the kitchen. It's all straight from brain to mouth.

So create with pure intent. Say what's on your mind, without filters or forethought, provided (and this is important) that it's not done at the expense of basic human respect. This Think Naked tactic may take you in directions contrary to accepted thinking. But when done with purity of intent, it will add to the wisdom of the world.

DOUBLE TALK

WHAT WE SAY	WHAT WE MEAN
In order to serve you better . . .	You're going to be inconvenienced.
What do you think?	You hate it, too, do you?
Let's review this.	I hate your work.
Have you tried . . .?	Start over.
Editing, by definition, is critical.	I'm going to mess with your work.
It's an interesting approach.	What in the hell were you thinking?

WHAT WE SAY	WHAT WE MEAN
Do these pants make me look fat?	I want to pick a fight.
Sure, I like pizza.	You stingy bastard.
I'm bored.	Let's have sex?
I feel your pain.	I'm glad it's you and not me.
Did you eat yet?	Do I have to feed you, too?
I'll call you later.	Good riddance.
It's not you, it's me.	I'm having an affair.
She's down to earth.	She's a horrible dresser.

CUT TO THE CHASE

Children know what they want and aren't inhibited when it comes to asking. They couldn't care less about practicality, propriety, or parliamentary procedure. But adults hem and haw. We lead into what we have to say and offer ideas in statements disguised as questions. When you think naked, you state what you want, plain and simple. Don't waste time dressing it up in fancy clothes. When we pad a request, we think we're negotiating when, really, we're wasting time.

Effective negotiation begins with a clear understanding of what you want. It's tough enough to negotiate when you know what you want, but it's almost impossible when you don't. People respect those who know what they want. We respect kids because they know what they want. Nobody can tell if you know what you want unless you can express it clearly, confidently, and even forcefully.

Even if you're not sure what you want, you know what you don't want. So at least express that much. Then take it from there and ask questions. You can turn any negotiation, deal making, bargain-making, or haggling session toward your favor with honest questions.

When negotiating for your personal needs, remember that your happiness is at stake. If you commit to something less than what you want, you'll not only be unhappy with the deal, you'll be unhappy with yourself. State your case clearly and confidently. It's okay to want the best for yourself.

MILK, MILK, LEMONADE

Okay, so you're going to cut to the chase, go with what's on your mind, straight from your gut. Sooner or later you're going to face expressing some delicate subjects. Your four-year-old genius can handle this. Did you ever hear this rhyme as a kid? "Milk, milk, lemonade, 'round the corner fudge is made."

I think I was six when I heard it—my first encounter with an acceptable way to express a taboo subject. Because the rhyme was silly and contained no real bad words, I was allowed to talk about breasts, urine, and excrement in one delicious rhyme. This technique is as old as the spoken word. Way back in the 14th century Geoffrey Chaucer dealt with all kinds of taboo subjects in *The Canterbury Tales.* This treasured work of English literature contains no less than ten references to *fart.* Setting the subject in a work of pure intent and presenting it humorously, Chaucer gets away with it.

Kids learn lots of gross stuff in a fun, song-like manner. They need to be introduced carefully to all of life's corners. Nursery rhymes and fairy tales helped all of us deal with the fear of parental separation, being lost, kidnapped, even the thought of death. Think of how terrifying it must have been to consider, "When the bough breaks, the baby will fall." In the same way, silly rhymes allow kids to exchange information about biological facts. (If we never even suggested to them that these subjects be taboo, they wouldn't need silly rhymes, but that's another story.)

Even adults feel apprehension or embarrassment discussing some subjects. Our comedians help us out. They can deal with all sorts of topics while performing under the cover of comedy. Jerry Seinfeld's show from the '90s often dramatized subjects people just don't talk about. We all ended up discussing them around the water cooler at work the day after the show. Funny, but when you give a taboo subject a smile, it becomes an acceptable subject. The next time you're faced with a tough subject (not just taboos) give it a smile J. Make it lyrical.

HABLA BLAH-BLAH

Kids may have invented language. We know that they keep improving it. They invent words all the time. English keeps stealing new words from other languages, new technologies, advertising and marketing, television and radio, writers and composers, but most of all from youth culture.

Some people complain about too many hip, new English words. Slang they call it. They forget how the language lives and grows. Academic eggheads want to control the language and keep it in their soft, little hands. I've seen this described as "fighting illiteracy." They forget that illiterates invented language. Think about it. The very first speakers had no language. They made it up. It was all slang. And by the time grammarians got a hold of it, language already had grammar, syntax, vocabulary, parts of speech, gender, mood, voice, tenses—all the crap that put us to sleep in English class—and the power to communicate. All the eggheads did was describe and organize what was already there. Okay, they can be the housekeepers of lingo. Fine. Just stay out of the way of the inventors who keep it fresh.

Most of the time new words describe better than old words what you're trying to say. Give me a phrase that better describes person-to-person interaction than *face time.* We need this new phrase today when so much other interaction is done without a face—telephone, e-mail, instant messaging, and fax. When no words you know will do, invent new ones. Try to beat the number *10* to describe an attractive person. In hip-hop terms he or she is "dime." What a vivid description of something that used to take a sentence to describe.

Someone who needed to say something no other words could describe invented every word we have. So why should you hesitate to invent words when you're at a loss for words? Today's hip, new words communicate to a large population. Some explain themselves—*chill*. Some you understand the first time you hear them in context. Like when somebody agrees with you saying, "I'm down with that." Or when a teenage girl sees something she likes and exclaims, "Sweet!"

New lingo serves another, important purpose. It builds solidarity among a select group. If you're not part of the group that easily refers to something cool as "off the hook," you shouldn't try to fake it. Not every woman will appreciate you calling her a dime or "phat." Not every man will respond as you hope if you greet him with, "Whazzup, dawg?" But there's still no need to let your vocabulary get old. New words can get you where you want to go in a fraction of the time it takes old words. Keep your ears open. Listen and choose your new words judiciously.

KID INVENTED WORDS

Bend the language. It's yours. Here's a list of phrases I've collected from my friends and family. Every one comes from a kid trying to describe something they either didn't know the name of or something that didn't have a name at the time.

KID EXPRESSION	MEANING
Poppy-poppy gun	Pneumatic jackhammer
Rainbow stains	Multicolored spots of light cast by the prisms of a cut-glass window
Gorilla cheese sandwich	Grilled cheese sandwich that enables you to climb like a gorilla
Dumb ask	Dumb question
Kitty antennas	Cat whiskers
Pee pee bat	Erection
It winded me	Strong gust of wind
Bah-doo-bee-doo	Ambulance
Butt burp	Flatulence
Hug the air	Substitute for hugging an absent loved one

Okay, hold on. This is really going to blow your mind. If you have any doubt about the natural beauty of creating new words, look at the list below. Then consider that all of them were invented by gorillas, Koko, Michael, and Ndume, at the Gorilla Foundation in California.

KID EXPRESSION	MEANING
Bottle match	Cigarette lighter
White tiger	Zebra
Eye hat	Face mask
Orange flower sauce	Nectarine yogurt
Bean ball	Peas
Elephant baby	Pinocchio doll
Bottle necklace	Plastic six-pack can holder

TELL ME A STORY

Imagine yourself snuggled in bed, freshly tucked in. Your mom or dad is about to tell you a story, probably your favorite story for the umpteenth time, or a new story—maybe from a brand new book, fresh with the scent of ink and paper. They could tell you a story about slimy, green frogs swimming in spaghetti and you'd love it. We all love a good story. The life of the party can hold your attention with stories that keep you hooked till the end.

If you're not so hot at telling stories, you probably wonder how a good storyteller does it. Well, you can buy books about how to tell a good story. But you can start telling better stories by practicing and learning from your successes and failures. In the end, though, any attempt at expressing yourself in a story will serve you better than merely laying out the cold, dry facts. Take something boring like a résumé and turn it into a story. Make it read like an adventure story even if all you did was sell vacuum cleaners. Give your story a hero, a conflict, and a resolution. Embellish and exaggerate the details. Tell or write your story with a smile on your face and comfort in your voice.

When you can't explain why something happens in your story, think like a kid. Using their imagination, children push their minds past reality to find explanations. You will, too, when push comes to shove. Practice making sensory details important. How can you look, listen, taste, smell, and use each seemingly irrelevant, innocuous piece of stimulus to create something fantastic and mesmerizing? Let your imagination take precedence over all other factors for a while.

LISTEN

A big part of expressing yourself requires that you do just the opposite. That's right, shut up and Listen. People shun unbearable bores that dominate conversations. Not because bores communicate too much. No, they communicate too little. Listening is the equal partner in all communication. It enhances your expression, because people Listen better to people who Listen to them. Listening allows you to guide your half of the conversation. You can't tell whether or not you're making yourself clear unless you check your feedback. We learn from listening with our hearts as well as our ears.

When people Listen to each other they build empathy. This is what it's all about—understanding each other's feelings, not just giving and receiving data. Computer networks do that. Only people gain empathy when they exchange data. We Listen for the underpinnings of how someone feels. We can see that when someone is crying or yelling or doing something desperate that it might be a cry for help and not always a malicious gesture.

Empathy is a gift we've all abused over time. We can and do take advantage of people when we see their weaknesses. Our ability to feel bad for the underdog sometimes gives way to our will to succeed at all costs. Like the little girl who automatically has to take home the crying, stray kitten, we have to regain our natural, kidlike tendency to feel for other people. We can't do this until we make a habit of listening.

POR FAVOR, SAY SOME MORE

In order to develop your listening and empathy skills, you may have to make a concerted effort at first, especially if you're a terrible listener. Here's an easy way to improve quickly. Every time you get the urge to interrupt someone and jump in with your two-cents worth, stop. Instead say, "Tell me more." Okay, that phrase will get real annoying real soon, so have some others ready.

Think like a news reporter. Some reporters use a simple technique—five Ws and an H. They ask *Who, What, When, Where, Why,* and *How?* That should keep you busy for a while. Why? (You're catching on!) Because it takes time to answer all those questions. These six questions fill out most of the dimensions of any statement. And you can easily convert them into more questions: How many, what for, why not, with whom, for how long . . .?

Some adults stop asking questions because they think they have all of the answers. We're afraid of looking stupid because we might ask the wrong question. Well, there are no wrong questions. Sometimes what sounds like the stupidest question leads to the greatest discovery. "Could we get to the Far East by sailing west?" The New World! When you stop asking questions, for whatever reason, you lose the opportunity to learn something new.

Unfortunately a group of high school students got just the opposite advice from United Supreme Court Justice Clarence Thomas in a live, question-and-answer session at their school. One inquisitive student, who obviously did his homework, asked Thomas why he didn't ask questions during oral arguments before the

Supreme Court. Thomas replied, "Usually, if you wait long enough, someone will ask your question." Sorry, Judge, but I can't think of worse advice!

Imagine you were one of the other kids at the Thomas talk—one of the other kids who wanted to ask him why he didn't ask questions. But you were afraid to ask, because you thought you'd sound stupid. Then Thomas makes his dimwitted reply. Now you feel doubly, doubly foolish! Not only could you have appeared sharper than a Supreme Court Justice, but also you missed a chance to be a hero to everyone who wanted to ask the same question. They all understand that if the kid who asked the question hadn't asked, it might have gone unasked. It's a brilliant question. And you could have asked it. Instead you feel as dumb as the judge. Not only that. Imagine how many kids suddenly realized, "If that clown can be a top judge, I sure can."

With his answer, Thomas proved the opposite of what he advised. Of course, someone might ask his question. But they might not. If he's doing his job, he should be formulating hard, probing questions based on his unique experience and expertise. Otherwise, he's redundant. The same goes for you in your life. You're here. You matter. All your questions are valid. You're not redundant. But you have to make yourself matter.

When you're not sure, ask a question. When you have no clue what someone is talking about, ask. It'll either buy you some time or give you a chance to understand what they're trying to convey. When you're looking for answers and you ask enough people, you'll find answers, solutions, and new ways to contemplate an issue. You'll never come away with less knowledge. Ask the president and the janitor and everyone in between about a subject. This will force you to communicate on lots of levels and will reveal many more layers of information.

Let your four-year-old genius ask the questions. I guarantee you'll get more and better information than ever. Kids aren't intellectual snobs, they're just curious. If they're not sure, they'll ask. Let the rest of the adult world dig in their heels defending their knuckle-headed opinions.

So much for fact gathering. The next step is even more important; it's the heart of empathy. You want to go deeper and learn, "How did that make you feel? What were you thinking? Did you like it? Was it awful?" You can make statements rather than questions. "I'm so happy for you. Let me help you. I'll bet that hurt! You must be proud of yourself."

Get people to talk and revelations occur. It may feel fake at first. As you get used to doing it and as you see how it improves not only your listening but also your expression, you'll start doing it naturally. And it will feel natural. It will work in business situations and in deeply personal ones. Your ability to listen when someone is screaming out, instead of getting defensive or considering it a personal attack, will not only bring the two of you closer, you'll both grow.

EMBARRASSMENT THRESHOLD

I'm sure a lot of academic work has been done that tells us why we get embarrassed and the physiology around getting embarrassed. You know, why we get that flush in our face. Why the sweaty palms and dilated pupils from doing or saying something we wish we hadn't. Why embarrassment?

The short answer—it's all about you. The more you dwell on yourself, the more likely you'll find something to embarrass you. You've heard of soldiers in the heat of battle taking a bullet to the arm or leg and not noticing it until the battle ends. Maybe you've bruised or cut yourself in a rough-and-tumble game, only to notice the damage afterward. It's much the same with performance. Musicians talk about being "in" the music, actors "in" their roles. When they are, they experience less stage fright and perform better.

Let's apply this to expressing yourself. When you concentrate on what you have to express, your mind doesn't have time to ask,

"What do they think of me?" Four-year-olds don't embarrass because they haven't set themselves up for it yet. They don't reflect on who they are and where they stand socially yet. They just get on with the fun. When was the last time you saw a kid blush about falling down? Just the opposite. They get up and fall down again on purpose.

We place a lot of emphasis on ourselves, our self-esteem, and satisfying our personal needs. We need to realize that all this attention opens us to a whole lot of disappointment and embarrassment. When we expect a lot of personal fulfillment, we set ourselves up for a lot of disappointment when we don't get it. On the other hand, if we concentrate on the work in front of us, on doing it well, we're more likely to do well. A lot of satisfaction comes from doing a job well, even if we don't get patted on the back.

What if we could assign a value or quantify embarrassment? We might be able to determine our personal threshold of embarrassment. Let's imagine a scale from one to ten. Ten—absolutely nothing embarrasses you. One—you blush whenever you hear your name. Call this scale your Embarrassment Threshold (ET).

I'm going to stick my neck out and say, the more you think about you and how you feel about what people think about you, the lower your ET will register. The more you think about other people and how they feel (empathy again), the higher your ET will rise. When you're expressing yourself and concerned with how you sound and what people think of you and what you're saying, the lower your ET. The more you begin to practice listening and working on making yourself clear, the higher your ET.

EXERCISE
Embarrassed? Me?

To get your ET as high as possible, start by focusing on what you do more than how you look. Focus on expressing rather than impressing. The next step—intentionally raising your ET by attacking embarrassing issues head-on. Here are a few things that tend to embarrass most people. If they seem threatening to you, good. Coax yourself into doing all the ones that might embarrass you. Then list some of your own and go to work on them.

- Tell someone you have a crush on them

- Sing in public

- Take dancing lessons

- Make up your own words and drop them into conversations

- Introduce yourself to a stranger in an elevator

- Ask a celebrity for an autograph

- Write a poem and recite it to a group of friends

ENGAGE AND DISTRIBUTE

Every moment offers you the opportunity to make a lasting impression on the lives of those around you. A smile, a warm glance, acknowledging people who help you or you see helping someone else—that's often all it takes to make a connection. Once you hook up, you can begin to exchange your DNA, the kind we talked about in Chapter 6. You distribute your Distinct Neuron Archetype and pick up some of theirs.

You're familiar with the theory that you're separated from anyone else in the world by less than six degrees of separation. I say it's more like two. Especially if you engage often. When you find yourself intrigued by someone, instead of just walking past them, engage. It's easy to engage. Just ask questions about the person you want to engage. Normal, healthy people love to talk about themselves. "Where'd you go to school? Have you ever been to . . .? What kind of music do you like?" And don't forget, "Hi! What's up?" Soon you'll build a network of associations that put you closer to anything you want or anybody you want to meet.

As you engage and distribute your unique personality, you'll learn more about yourself. Remember my Sandbox City story in Chapter 4? Just looking back on it illustrates to me how kids engage each other with instinctual trust. It happened decades ago and now it's a story in my book. But as we mature, we separate ourselves by social status, language, education, geography, and our prejudices. To counter that, I make a habit of engaging people who catch my attention. And many do. One way or the other. I don't always know why—a moment of eye contact, a smile, they're wearing great shoes. I just go with my gut. I trust my hunches. And it has paid off over and over again. Often with amazing results. I know my best friends, my former wife, Andre 3000, Tommie Smith, most of the people I work with, and my publisher because I consciously and sometimes aggressively engaged.

That's why I engage people on the street, in airports, and on the phone. Yes, I even engage telephone solicitors. (You'd be surprised how fast they end the call when they realize you're try- ing to get something from them!) I'm always amazed at what great connections I make from random meetings. I'm even more amazed when I think what I'd miss if I didn't engage. So many of my best opportunities come directly from someone I took the time to meet and engage in conversation.

I started this chapter with a story about Tommie Smith. He's been a hero of mine since he made his courageous statement to the world in 1968. Because I make a habit of engaging, I got to meet him. It took more than one call. I won't tell you how many. He's a busy man with good reason to screen his callers. But I per- sisted and eventually had dinner with him and his wife. I can only begin to tell you how meeting him has strengthened my resolve.

Think back in your own life. How you met someone you came to love. What if you hadn't said hello? What if you hadn't called back? They say opportunity knocks only once, but I say most of the time you have to knock. Or say hello, offer a hand, start a con- versation. When you do this more often, you multiply your chances of meeting someone who may know someone who will offer you a better job. Make you a better deal. Maybe introduce you to your soul mate. Heck, could even be your soul mate.

Now you've got a lot of tools and advice on how to express yourself. The opportunities to do so will come. They're every- where. Ever notice that when you buy a car, all of a sudden you see that kind of car more often on the road? The same thing's going to happen—once you decide to express yourself better and more often, you'll see your openings more clearly. I don't know why it works this way; I can only promise you that it does. And that engaging and distributing will make your life more exciting.

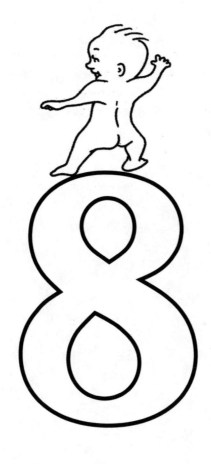

I'M THE BOSS OF ME

To _____ ☐ **URGENT**
                                    A.M.
Date_____Time_____ P.M.
WHILE YOU WERE OUT
From_____YOU FORGOT_____
Message_____

Ideas are only as good
as your ability
to make them happen.

— MARIO MARSAN,
Signed___ MY DAD AND OWNER OF 22 U.S. AND
INTERNATIONAL PATENTS

001 Reorder No.

Y ou've just read seven chapters of a book that pretty much tells you what to do. Now I want to make sure I completely reverse that attitude. As the title of this chapter clearly states, you're in charge. I can't make you do anything. That means you have to tell yourself what to do from now on.

This book, the ideas, principles, and ideals it stands for are totally worthless unless they become a part of your life. That's 365 days a year. Think about it. You've got a lot of catching up to do. And it's going to take more than just nodding your head at this point to make naked thinking the positive, hope-giving, life-changing force it can be.

You bought this book and you've read this far. You've started to make your environment alive with the vital stimulation of people who provide a variety of thinking styles. You support your peers and get support in return. You stack the deck for success. You might even have started to express yourself more often. It feels better than sitting on your hands with no opinion, doesn't it? Shouldn't this be enough to motivate you to make naked thinking a part of your life? No!

No

There's that word again! Throughout your life, over a 10-, 20-, 30-, 40-year period, at least 15 to 40 times a day you've heard the word No. Do the math. That word, repeated that many times, can be more debilitating than the Chinese water torture. Worse, because it's never going to end, even when you clearly understand that the word No is someone else's problem, not your life sentence. Even when you realize that naysayers fear your success and that their *noes* are just the hurdles they throw in your way. Even then, No still does its damage. Hear it enough and it's so easy to conclude, "There's no hope!" Most of us have come to that conclusion more than once in our lives.

Medical studies are more and more conclusive—hope keeps us alive! Patients with hope have a higher survival rate than those given a grim prognosis. We're so much into toughing things out that we don't realize the value of giving someone a fighting chance. Do you ever want to just fade away? Not me. I want to go down fighting like Paul Newman's character in *Cool Hand Luke*. Even if I don't stand a chance, fighting will give me a sense of purpose. At least while you're fighting, you still have hope.

Yes

There was a time when if someone told you no, your resolve would strengthen. That's where you want to be again. Likewise, you want to say Yes as often as possible. If you've read anything into this book, you understand it's not just about you. It's about nurturing naked thinking in the rest of the world, if only for your own sake. The more naked thinkers, the easier it will be for all of us to think naked. Say *Yes* to your spirited, walk-to-their-own-beat employees or coworkers. *Yes* to your kids and teens during their most critical years of development. Say *Yes* to the naked thinkers who preceded us.

People will always project their negative feelings in an effort to deal with their own issues. They'll still use judgmental language with you because they're judging themselves. Don't take it personally. Give them a little eye roll, the same one you gave to a scolding parent or adult when you were three years old. The look that said, "Mom, I'm busy building this sandcastle and pretending I'm an aardvark." Get in the habit of saying, "Yes!"

WHY

Sometimes people listen to what I say and tell me, "That sounds smart." I'd rather hear, "Why?" So I'll just pretend that when you put down this book, you're going to use every last drop of your kid-like curiosity. Before you do, you want to know why one more time. You've read all the rational reasons. You've checked my claims from the science I've cited. But you want a real, gut-level answer to why. Instead of asking why, ask why three times like you learned in Chapter 6.

> *I didn't want to skate for a gold medal. I went out and had a great time.*
>
> — SARAH HUGHES,
> Gold Medalist,
> Women's Singles Skating,
> 2002 Winter Olympics

WHY?
Because you were once a little genius.

WHY?
Because your genius is not irreversible.

WHY?
Because your life experience and education
puts you in the best position ever in
to have a great life.

In our Big Idea Sessions at Marco Polo Explorers, some people do what I tell them to do because it sounds smart. When they do it for rational reasons, they miss the feeling they'd get if they let it hit them on a more visceral level. I once told a very pragmatic client that studies proved when you're having fun, you're more likely to create breakthrough ideas. Within two minutes he was whipping Nerf balls at people, laughing kind of nervously, "We're having fun, fun, fun!" He knew it was smart and he was doing it because it was smart. He missed the point—chill, have fun, and check the results at the end of the process instead of trying to affect it every second. None of this will make sense unless it becomes organic and natural.

Throw Nerf balls only if it's you. Do it because it feels better. Do it to lose touch with your troubles. Children do all these things because they feel good. That's why ball-tossing works. There's no connection between throwing balls and breakthrough thinking. Only between fun and breakthrough thinking. So if throwing balls isn't fun for you, have fun some other way. Call balls and strikes. Cheer the ball throwers. Or boo them. Intercept a pass. Make sound effects, or do the play-by-play. Do it in another language or Pig Latin. Be the Goodyear blimp. Just have fun, keep having fun, revel in the ideas that come, and scream with glee when you discover something really new and exciting.

Okay, we've sort of got our ducks in a row now. I've just laid out the basic formula for making the four Think Naked principles part of your life. Let's do a quick review of those principals. Then I'll give you a fiery battle cry about Choice, Commitment, and the Naked Reflex.

WEAR YOUR CAPE

Create an environment, a way of talking to people, a way of treating yourself that feels safe—envelope yourself, your team, and your family with unconditional respect. Give them the opportunity to take chances. Build a safety net to protect anyone who takes a chance and wants to express outrageous ideas, be wrong, and even fail. Nurture the courage it takes to volunteer a thought or an idea a new way. Exercise an unconditional will to listen, nurture, and to respect everyone's input.

BLOCKBUSTER

When a belief becomes so ingrained that it starts to debilitate you, bust it. Heck, get good at blockbusting and you'll bust blocks before they get ingrained. Develop your deficiencies into assets. Break stereotypes, systematically. Challenge the natural physiology that makes your thinking slow down and repeat itself. You can't avoid the fact that you become hardwired by age 12, but you can bust up your hardwiring. Remember the nuns of Mankato and keep learning until the day you die.

LOOK AT YOUR NEIGHBOR'S PAPER

Toss out the idea that you're the smartest person on the planet. You're not. Forget the "no pain, no gain" martyr mantra. Why tough it out? Cheat! Not on your SATs, taxes, or your spouse. But do get help when you need it. Value the learning that precedes you. Make friends and build alliances with people who know more than you do. Find stimulus that's done some of the work for you. The kind of stimulation that has intelligence built in. Learn how to identify the traits that separate a Pez dispenser from an ordinary candy package. Always ask more than one person for directions. Always generate lots of ideas instead of just one that works.

SHOW-N-TELL

And for God's sake, express yourself! Be true to the amazing exuberance you've suppressed for years and years. Engage the people you meet and distribute your true, naked thinking self at all times. No more "would've, could've, should've!" Unload all the excuses you use now. All of those self-limiting behaviors that keep you from experiencing all you were meant to experience, all the people you were meant to meet, and the girl or guy you should have married. Use your childlike innocence to raise your embarrassment threshold to ten or higher—through the roof! Nobody needs nonchalant, fake cool. And everybody sees through it.

See Saw

Most importantly, remember the rule of balance I illustrated with the playground seesaw. Without the wisdom of your life experience and knowledge base, the four Think Naked principles will make you childish rather than childlike. You'll be acting like a four-year-old instead of thinking like one.

The previous four paragraphs merely summarize their respective chapters. Go back and review the chapters when you find yourself starting to think like an uptight, big shot adult. Keep the adult part that makes you a loving, nurturing, responsible spouse, parent, and contributing member of society. Keep your adult passions for mental and spiritual growth. Just let your four-year-old genius drive them.

Choice

It's time to revisit the promise I made in chapter one. I promised more opportunities in your future and eventually greater fulfillment in your life and relationships and ultimately a life free of despair. But under the heading "Help Yourself," I told you that you need to make a choice to make naked thinking a way of life—not just once, but every day with every step you take.

When you're more aware of every single step you take, you realize that every moment offers you a choice. Rare moments bring you to a major crossroad. But you make many smaller choices every day. When someone cuts you off in traffic, you make a choice—obscene gesture or, "All right, go ahead. You must be in an awful hurry." When you walk through any door, you choose to keep going or hold it open for the person following you. Every time you meet a friend, you decide how to greet them. Will it be a "Hi!" a handshake, or a hug this time?

These smaller, everyday choices add up and make an even greater impact on your life than the major choices. It makes sense, then, to pay more attention to your daily and hourly choices. Nothing long lasting and worthwhile happens overnight. You have to commit to the long haul. So it may take a long distance point of view, a humble sense of your place in the universe to keep making the right choices.

When you start to take a bird's eye view of the world, you understand just how hard it is to stand out or to make a difference. You start to understand your relative insignificance in the world and then, *Bammm*! It hits you, and you say to yourself, "The only way I can be significant is to make significant things happen. Do the significant things that will make me stand out in the eyes of my family, my peers, and the planet. When everyone else is caught up in the insignificance, I will stand out, with a smile, an alternative suggestion, a fresh new way." Once you say this, when you know in your heart of hearts that you are only here for a relatively short time, you become more directed, more determined to make a difference in this world. Making more directed choices.

Here's one of the toughest choices you're going to have to make, though. If thinking naked is radically different from the way you've been living, you need to send your negative, sullen, pragmatist mindset into solitary confinement. It's time to change the way you think at its very foundation.

You've got to make it happen. Nobody else. You. It's your choice, just as it was your choice early in life to start leaving your little genius behind. You chose to leave your genius behind, but only because you trusted the wisdom of the world that preceded you. You're smarter now. You've read the book. You know that adults were undermining your genius, because they didn't think they had a choice. They were doing what they were told. They were toughing it out, and you trusted them. Now that you know this, you need to choose otherwise.

You've got to *make it happen*. Today! You've got to change the culture you're living in to lead your family, your team, and yourself back to the place where big thoughts abound and being wrong sounds like being right.

WHY IS WILLIE A WINO?

Because he's made the same bad choices. Not just one bad choice the day he decided to become a wino. In fact, he never decided to become a wino. He made a series of bad choices—not to go work one day, not to show up for a job interview another day. He decided to stay at the bar another hour, to have another drink, and another, and another. He decided not to get help when it looked like he was hitting the skids. He passed up help on his way to another drink. Willie makes a series of bad choices, back to back to back, every day of his life. The wrong choices get easier and the right ones get that much harder, but he still makes choices every waking hour.

TRUE   FAKE

COMMITMENT

It's easy choosing to think naked one time or two times. Staying committed, that's where the numbers drop. Thinking naked requires constant choices. In a word—commitment. First you have to break the cycle of bad choices—failing to treat your ideas and the ideas of others with respect, toughing it out when you could get help, accepting stereotypes, copping an excuse, fading into the background when you have the opportunity to engage. You've got to stop. Not just once a day but every minute. Recognize your new way of processing. Acknowledge it out loud. The next time you create a solution based on your newfound skill, let people know you were thinking naked.

The road to hell
is paved
with good intentions.

— SAMUEL JOHNSON

Take heart. It gets easier. Each time you choose not to follow an old pattern, you're actually making smarter choices instead. Gradually, naked thinking becomes a habit, but only if you commit yourself and repeat great choices. Time and time again. It helps to keep your High Concept in mind. Maybe even over your desk or on your night stand. I once asked someone who bragged about having a mantra what it was? He couldn't remember! Well then, it wasn't a mantra, was it? Your High Concept is your mantra. It's no good if you forget it. So repeat it every day, especially when thinking naked seems difficult.

RUNNING FOR HER LIFE

In the hills of Tennessee, a little girl was born into the direst poverty, the seventeenth of nineteen children. When she was four she suffered an attack of scarlet fever that paralyzed her left leg. Doctors said she would be disabled for the rest of her life. End of story, right?

Not quite. The little girl wanted to run more than anything else in the world. When she was six, she began hopping around on her one good leg. She was getting around but it was awkward. She knew she wasn't normal, so she worked harder. Slowly she began to make progress. When she was eight and fitted with a brace she began to walk, uncertain at first, but she got around. This is the same girl who years ago had been relegated to a life of despair.

As she grew older, she invented games to take her mind off of the constant discomfort of attempting to run. Soon she was running, slowly and awkwardly, but she was running. In her own way she had made a choice to run and had committed herself to that end goal—daily, hourly, into her teens. Then one day, she ran.

Ten years later and all grown up, *Time* magazine wrote of her, "From the moment she first sped down the track in Rome's Olympic Stadium, there was no doubt she was the fastest woman the world had ever seen." The little girl was Wilma Rudolph, the world's fastest woman. She had conquered despair with hope. And hope gave her control over the outcome of her life.

GUILT 101

Some people don't react well to positive coaching until they read about someone like Wilma Rudolph. But if even that's not enough to keep you committed to naked thinking, here's a fall back plan—guilt. I'm of Italian descent and know just how powerful and effective guilt can be. It can be anything from a sort of string around your finger or a horrible, debilitating weight around your neck. But what if we turn guilt on its head? Instead of feeling sick with guilt, just prod ourselves with guilty reminders.

I want you to feel at least a little poke of guilt whenever you get too full of yourself and make a big deal over something that's not going to affect the world. For example? When you make someone feel bad, because you go after him or her like a big, boneheaded adult. When you snap at your spouse or kids before you really listen.

THE NAKED REFLEX

For this book to truly have value, you need to think naked without thinking twice. To do that, you have to develop the Naked Reflex. With the Naked Reflex you no longer have to ponder your choices. When challenged with a problem, you'll come up with brilliant solutions and new opportunities automatically. But in order to develop this reflex, you have to exercise your brain on a regular basis and make naked thinking choices every minute of every day.

> Chance favors only the prepared mind.
> — LOUIS PASTEUR

The Naked Reflex is an advanced form of naked thinking. Don't just assume, having read this section, that you've developed it. You'll feel the reflex when you notice a consistency of choice that adds up to a daily winning streak.

When you exercise regularly, no matter what kind of ability you're trying to develop or improve, you stack the deck in your favor. You eliminate a lot of the chance life typically tosses your way and start to systematically reduce the possibility of downside. That's why you should try to do as much of what I recommend as possible. Each of the principles in the book works in concert with the others. I know that some of them will make more sense and appeal to you more than others. But I assure you that the cumulative effect of all practicing of them, when you incorporate them into your life, will make you happier and free from daily anguish.

Like a diet, you can think naked for a week or ten weeks and temporarily lose your bad thinking habits. But the rewards will be temporary. I don't want you to do this. I want you to embrace the Think Naked way of life. Like everyday exercise, you will be much better off; you will create profound improvement in your life. This way of life made you a genius when you were four years old. It can do even more for you now, fed by the wealth of your life's experience.

Please go back and read the book again within the next two to three weeks. Practice the principles, put them in motion. As you make the transition, take your time or do it quickly, but don't let any more time go by. Get on with it.

When expressing yourself gets you "The Look," say, "Sorry. I'm a Repeat Offender." Tell anyone who gives you "The Look" that you're thinking naked. Watch their reaction. Turn it into a chance to bring another naked thinker into the fold. When you think you've got someone interested, send him or her a Brain Wedgie—a thought that will change the way they think forever. Then give the book to someone else. Show them your commitment to thinking naked.

Equip yourself for the ever-changing world. Rid yourself of embarrassment. Have pride in what you and your God have put on this planet. You. There's only one you. And now it's the you as the genius you once were.

Look out, planet Earth . . .

Here comes _____[your name here]_____ /

> It is not the strongest
> of the species that survive,
> nor the most intelligent,
> but the one most responsive
> to change.
>
> — CHARLES DARWIN

THINK NAKED WORKSHEET

*U*se this worksheet to guide your thinking through the Think Naked process. I've included all the examples I've charted in the book.

- Describe what you want to accomplish in the

- Challenge column. List as many people, tools, resources, as well as your own experience and abilities, in the See column.

- Select one or more Think Naked techniques from the Saw column.

- Apply your See and Saw to your Challenge, and get ready for a great, unexpected solution.

CHALLENGE	SEE	SAW	RESULT
WHAT YOU WANT TO ACCOMPLISH	WHAT YOU HAVE AT YOUR DISPOSAL	THINK NAKED TECHNIQUE	UNEXPECTED SOLUTION
		WEAR YOUR CAPE Happy Place Monster Under the Bed Go Down Swinging Sandbox City Fear in Your Back Pocket Support First Get the Look Discount and Revenge **BLOCKBUSTER** Wow! It's A Cow! Freshness Dating Space Out A Day in the Life If It Ain't Broke, Break It Brain Wedgies	

CHALLENGE	SEE	SAW	RESULT
WHAT YOU WANT TO ACCOMPLISH	WHAT YOU HAVE AT YOUR DISPOSAL	THINK NAKED TECHNIQUE	UNEXPECTED SOLUTION
		LOOK AT YOUR NEIGHBOR'S PAPER *Life Is an Open-Book Test* *Why, Why, Why* *His Truck Is Better* *Double It or Add a Zero* *DNA* *Dress Up* *Let the Force Be with You* *Trip to the Zoo* *Square Peg, Round Hole* *Uberkid* **SHOW-N-TELL** *I Wanna Be a Fire Fighter* *High Concept* *Blue Suns, Yellow Skies* *Naked Barbie* *Play-Doh Possibilities* *No Shame in Your Game* *For Cryin' Out Loud!* *Repeat Offender* *Cut to the Chase*	

CHALLENGE	SEE	SAW	RESULT
Find an antidote for mustard gas	Mustard gas efficiently kills lymph cells and white blood cells	Wow! It's a Cow!	Cancer-fighting drug
Remove cockleburs	Microscopic hooks	Wow! It's a Cow!	Velcro
Stop washing interruptions	How to engineer solutions	A Day in the Life	Bounce
Generate electricity	Wateralls	Let the Force Be with You	Hydroelectric power
Prevent rust	Beetle's tiny water channels	Trip to the Zoo	Automotive water drainage
Prevent door from slamming	Tennis ball, twine, nail, or screw	Let the Force Be with You	Swinging-ball door-slam suppressor
Prevent hand burns	Inadequate faucet design	For Cryin' Out Loud	Single-handle mixing faucet

WHILE YOU WERE OUT

To _____

☐ **URGENT**

A.M.
P.M.

Date _____ Time _____

From _____ YOU FORGOT _____

Message _____
Fairy tales can come true,
it can happen to you
If you're young at heart
For it's hard, you will find,
to be narrow of mind
If you're young at heart

Signed JOHNNY RICHARDS & CAROLYN LEIGH,
Young at Heart

001 Reorder No.

ABOUT THE AUTHOR

Marco Marsan, master corporate creativity expert and founder of renowned think tank Marco Polo Explorers, is regarded as one of America's most inventive minds.

Selected by Mazda Corporation as one of their top Out-of-the-Box Thinkers, he has worked with over 200 of the Fortune 500 companies over the last decade. Clients include Nike, Gatorade, Neutrogena, AT&T, Procter & Gamble, General Mills, Kimberly-Clark, and Pepsi.

In more than 500 high-intensity *Big Idea! Sessions,* Marco has honed his radical ideation techniques to give his clients an unbeatable edge. Marco has spoken to tens of thousands of people on the power of innovation and creativity at his speaking engagements. Author, marketer, corporate anarchist, and entrepreneur, Marsan lives with his son, Shane, in the majestic Appalachian foothills of Mt. Lookout, Ohio. He has been seen as a guest on *The View* with Barbara Walters, and *The Montel Williams Show.*

You may contact Marco direct at
marco@thinknaked.com

To find more information about
Marco Polo Explorers, go to
www.marcopoloexplorers.com

MONEY-BACK GUARANTEE

Don't ponder any longer. Either agree with what I'm asking you to do and make something happen or disagree with me and get your money back. I'm not going to let you off that easy though. Here's what it takes to get your money back:

Send me your compelling argument for why you can't or won't start thinking naked. Why you want to wallow in a world of despair, and why having fun isn't what you want in life. I'll personally send you your money back and use your comments to start a new book, *1001 Reasons to Live in Despair*. I hope I don't hear from more than 1001 people or the title won't work.

This guarantee comes directly from me. So don't bother the publisher for your money back. I take full responsibility. Send your arguments to **1001@thinknaked.com**.